The "Natural Inferiority" of Women

.

Outrageous Pronouncements by Misguided Males

COMPILED BY

Tama Starr

POSEIDON PRESS   NEW YORK   LONDON   TORONTO   SYDNEY   TOKYO   SINGAPORE

POSEIDON PRESS
SIMON & SCHUSTER BUILDING
ROCKEFELLER CENTER
1230 AVENUE OF THE AMERICAS
NEW YORK, NEW YORK 10020

POSEIDON PRESS IS A REGISTERED TRADEMARK OF SIMON & SCHUSTER INC.
POSEIDON PRESS COLOPHON IS A TRADEMARK OF SIMON & SCHUSTER INC.

DESIGNED BY KAROLINA HARRIS
MANUFACTURED IN THE UNITED STATES OF AMERICA

1 3 5 7 9 10 8 6 4 2

LIBRARY OF CONGRESS CATALOGING-IN-PUBLICATION DATA
THE "NATURAL INFERIORITY" OF WOMEN : OUTRAGEOUS PRONOUNCEMENTS BY MISGUIDED MALES/
COMPILED BY TAMA STARR.
P.   CM.
INCLUDES INDEX.
1. WOMEN—QUOTATIONS, MAXIMS, ETC. I. STARR, TAMA.
PN6084.W6N37   1991
305.42—DC20   91-24212
CIP
ISBN: 0-671-74431-3

To my father
Mel Starr
(1919–1988)

Contents

PART TWO: DOMESTICATING THE FEMALE

Non possunt invectivae omnes, et satirae
in feminas scriptae, uno volumine comprehendi.

(One volume could never contain
All the insults and satires against women.)

—CRISTOVAL DE FONSECA, *DEVOUT CONTEMPLATIONS* (1614)

Introduction

Great Men through the ages, whatever their other persuasions, concur with startling unanimity on woman's "natural" inferiority to Man. No other thesis finds such disparate personalities as Buddha and Nietzsche, Confucius and Darwin in such ardent accord. What has never before been recognized, however, is that the Theory of Female Inferiority is in itself a coherent philosophy: as rational as the minds that embrace it, as convincing as the premises it is based upon, and as logical and ingenious as anything the Marx Brothers ever devised.

Here, in the authentic words of its most lucid proponents, is the complete Theory of Female Inferiority, arranged and presented so clearly that even a woman can understand it. In more than six hundred eloquent quotations—from peasants' proverbs to emperors' edicts—a host of impassioned patriarchs will demonstrate the masculine reasoning process by explaining exactly how and why women are inferior to men.

From the simplest characterizations of the female as alien beast to the most elaborate programs for subjugating her, the male-superior philosophy has a logic all its own. If one accepts the premises and surrenders to the reasoning, the rest inevitably follows.

This uniquely successful doctrine has captivated the world, informing religion, philosophy, literature, and law. Why, one may reasonably wonder, if women really are inferior to men, should it be necessary for men to keep saying so—and with such feverish persistence? But the male-superior philosophy clearly meets a need. After all, if two sexes exist, isn't one necessarily "better" than the other?

Only by stepping outside the system to view the argument whole can we appreciate the amazing circular reasoning that distinguishes this dazzling ideology.

Every effort has been made to respect the integrity of the argument and the masters who propound it. The savants and sages whose thoughts constitute the core of this book have been given a fair opportunity to present their case. While statements by fictional characters are also included, as dynamic expressions of the beliefs of their times, such statements are attributed to the characters themselves, not to their creators.

The outstanding feature of this fantastic philosophy is that it is still in force after five thousand years. Readers can decide for themselves the validity, worth, and future of the Theory of Female Inferiority. Examining it objectively will provide, at the very least, fun for feminists, malaise to masculists, ammunition to those in search of a joke on the little woman, outrage to many, and food for thought to anyone who is intrigued by the ironies of the war between the sexes.

The "Natural Inferiority" of Women

Part One

Evil
Is
Woman

SINCE WOMAN IS MAN'S OPPOSITE,
AND MAN, WE KNOW, IS GOOD,
WOMAN MUST BE EVIL.

What Is Woman?

Let us begin with some simple definitions of the female beast.

The first observation that springs to Man's mind is of woman's ineffable Otherness.

But it was given to Adam to "name the animals": to achieve mastery over alien beings by categorizing them and putting them in their place. And so did Adam's sons attempt to do with women.

■ *What is woman?*

. . . man's confusion.

—GREEK AND LATIN PROVERBS

. . . a shrew in the kitchen, a saint in the church, an angel at the board, and an ape in the bed.

—ENGLISH PROVERB (16TH CENTURY)

. . . an inferior man.

—ARISTOTLE, *POETICS* (323 B.C.)

. . . a softer Man.

—ALEXANDER POPE, "OF THE CHARACTERS OF WOMEN" (1732–33)

. . . a promise that cannot be kept.

—PAUL CLAUDEL (ca. 1920)

What else is a woman but a foe to friendship, a cosmic punishment, a necessary evil, a natural temptation, a desirable calamity, a domestic peril, a delectable detriment, a deadly fascination, a painted ill! Therefore, if it be a sin to divorce her when she ought to be kept, it is indeed a necessary torture; for either we commit adultery by divorcing her, or we must endure daily strife.

—ST. JOHN CHRYSOSTOM (ca. A.D. 380)

Women are necessary evils.

—ENGLISH PROVERB (16TH CENTURY); GREEK, LATIN, AND SLOVENIAN PROVERBS

. . . sphinxes without secrets.

—DORIAN GRAY IN OSCAR WILDE, *PICTURE OF DORIAN GRAY* (1891)

. . . made of nectar and poison.

—ARABIC PROVERB

. . . silver dishes into which we put golden apples.

—JOHANN WOLFGANG VON GOETHE, *CONVERSATIONS WITH ECKERMANN* (1823)

. . . sweetly smiling angels with pensive looks, innocent faces, and cash-boxes for hearts.

—HONORÉ DE BALZAC, *COUSIN BETTE* (1846)

■ *Women, it seems, are full of contradictions.*

If long, she is lazy;
If little, she is loud;
If fair, she is sluttish;
If foul, she is proud.

—JOHN FLORIO, *SECOND FRUTES* (1591)

. . . You are pictures out of doors,
Bells in your parlors, wild-cats in your kitchens,
Saints in your injuries, devils being offended,
Players in your housewifery, and housewives in your beds.

—IAGO IN WILLIAM SHAKESPEARE, *OTHELLO* (1604)

A woman has the form of an angel, the heart of a serpent, and the mind of an ass.

—GERMAN PROVERB

■ *Man's confusion is understandable.*

Woman is as hard to know as a melon.

—SPANISH PROVERB

Woman's nature flutters this way and that, and it is hard to serve her.
She is more difficult to understand than the wisest words of the sages.

—A SAGE IN THE *RÂMÂYANA* (ca. 500 B.C.)

Women are like tricks by sleight of hand,
Which, to admire, we should not understand.

—VALENTINE IN WILLIAM CONGREVE, *LOVE FOR LOVE* (1689)

■ *Incomprehensible as these beings may be, Man bears the burden of
their care and feeding.*

Women are like elephants to me: nice to look at, but I wouldn't want
to own one.

—W. C. FIELDS (ca. 1935)

He that taketh a wife getteth a possession.

—APOCRYPHA, ECCLESIASTICUS 26:3 (ca. 200 B.C.)

Women are like baggage.

—A. C. BHAKTIVEDANTA SWAMI (1970)

Women are the baggage of life: they are troublesome, and hinder us in
the great march, and yet we cannot be without 'em.

—GRAINEVERT IN SIR JOHN SUCKLING, *BRENNORALT* (1646)

He that keeps a wife is like he that keeps a monkey: he is responsible for her mischief.

—ENGLISH LEGAL PROVERB

A good woman is like a good book—entertaining, inspiring, and instructive; sometimes a bit too wordy, but when properly bound and decorated, irresistible. I wish I could afford a library.

—MARCUS LONG, ONTARIO LIBRARY REVIEW (1971)

Ugly wives and stupid maids are priceless treasures.

—CHINESE PROVERB

If my wife cheated, I'd kill her. She's part of my property. I feel I *own* her, the way I own my car. And I don't lend my car.

—AL GOLDSTEIN, AMERICAN PUBLISHER (1973)

I will be the master of what is mine own:
She is my goods, my chattels; she is my house,
My household stuff, my field, my barn,
My horse, my ox, my ass, my anything.

—PETRUCHIO IN WILLIAM SHAKESPEARE, THE TAMING OF THE SHREW (1594)

■ *Females do possess a certain utility.*

First house and wife and an ox for the plough.

—HESIOD, WORKS AND DAYS (ca. 800 B.C.)

Women are created for work. One of them can draw or carry as much as two men. They also pitch our tents, make our clothes, mend them, and keep us warm at night. . . . We absolutely cannot get along without them on a journey. They do everything and cost only a little; for since they must be forever cooking, they can be satisfied in lean times by licking their fingers.

—A CHIPPEWA CHIEF (1930)

Wife: a handy little item you can screw on the bed that does all the work.

—AMERICAN JOKE (ca. 1970)

My wife is my mule.

—MONTENEGRIN PROVERB

■ *It seems reasonable to classify human females with the other beasts that share Man's world.*

An animal usually living in the vicinity of man and having a rudimentary susceptibility to domestication . . . the woman is lithe and graceful in its movements, is omnivorous and can be taught not to talk.

—AMBROSE BIERCE, *THE DEVIL'S DICTIONARY* (1906)

A woman is but an animal, and not an animal of the highest order.

—EDMUND BURKE, *REFLECTIONS ON THE REVOLUTION IN FRANCE* (1756)

. . . an animal that delights in finery.

—JOSEPH ADDISON, *THE SPECTATOR* (JANUARY 3, 1712)

. . . a milk-white lamb that bleats for man's protection.

—JOHN KEATS, "ENDYMION" (1818)

A wife, like a dog, is sought for her race-breed.

—CUBAN PROVERB

Women are troublesome cattle to deal with mostly.

—GOGGINS IN SAMUEL LOVER, *HANDY ANDY* (1842)

Where you find a cow you find a woman; and where you find a woman you find bother.

—IRISH PROVERB

Women are like *Flies,* which feed among us at our Table; or *Fleas* sucking our very blood, who leave not our most retired places free from their familiarity, yet for all their fellowship will they never be tamed nor commanded by us.

—JOHN DONNE, *PROBLEMS AND PARADOXES* (1603–9)

. . . glow wormes bright
that soil our soules, and dampe our reasons light.
—JOHN MARSTON, *THE SCOURGE OF VILLANIE* (1598)

■ *Still, it may be nobler to think of women as belonging to a higher order of life than the insect.*

Man is the hunter; woman is his game:
The sleek and shining creatures of the chase,
We hunt them for the beauty of their skins;
They love us for it, and we ride them down.
—ALFRED, LORD TENNYSON, "THE PRINCESS" (1847)

Three women and a goose make a market.
—DANISH, ITALIAN, AND POLISH PROVERBS

Where there are women and geese, there wants no noise.
—ENGLISH PROVERB

The goose bends its head while walking, but its eyes wander.
—TALMUD, MEGILLAH 14B (ca. A.D. 300)

■ *The very discerning may be able to distinguish among the various types and characteristics of the female beast:*

Woman is like three things: wolf, fox, and cat.
Wolf, fox, and cat are beasts of prey:
Cat seeks, fox waits, wolf rends and tears.

—JEAN DE MEUNG, *ROMAN DE LA ROSE* (13TH CENTURY)

In the beginning God made woman apart from man.

One made He of a bristly Sow; all that is in her house lies disorderly, defiled with dirt, and rolling upon the floor, and she groweth fat sitting among the middens [garbage] in garments as unwashed as herself.

Another of a Bitch, a busybody like her mother . . . [who] barketh e'en though she see nothing; a man cannot check her with threats, no, not if in anger he dash her teeth out with a stone, nor yet though he speak gently with her, even though she be sitting among strangers— she must needs keep up her idle baying. . . .

Another's made of a stubborn and belaboured She-Ass; everything she doeth is hardly done, of necessity and after threats, and then 'tis left unfinished; meanwhile eateth she day in day out, in bower and in hall, and all men alike are welcome to her bed.

Another of a Cat, a woeful and miserable sort . . . she is mad for a love-mate, and yet when she hath him turneth his stomach. . . .

Another cometh of an Ape; she is the greatest ill of all. . . . Alas for the wretched man that claspeth such a mischief! Like an ape she knoweth all arts and wiles. . . .

—SEMONIDES OF AMORGOS, *IAMBI* (ca. 660 B.C.)

Like all young men, you greatly exaggerate the difference between one young woman and another.

—UNDERSHAFT IN GEORGE BERNARD SHAW, *MAJOR BARBARA* (1905)

■ *Many thinkers have commented on women's interchangeability.*

When the candles are out, all cats are gray.
—ENGLISH PROVERB (16TH CENTURY); SIMILARLY: BOSNIAN, GREEK, AND LATIN PROVERBS

One crack is as good as another and over every sewer there's a grating.
—HENRY MILLER, *BLACK SPRING* (1963)

Wicked women bother one. Good women bore one. That is the only difference between them.
—CECIL GRAHAM IN OSCAR WILDE, *LADY WINDERMERE'S FAN* (1892)

So-called decent women differ from whores mainly in that whores are less dishonest.
—LEO TOLSTOY, *THE KREUTZER SONATA* (1899)

Most women have no characters at all.
—ALEXANDER POPE, "OF THE CHARACTERS OF WOMEN" (1732–33)

Human nature being twofold, the better sort should henceforth be called "man."
—PLATO, *TIMAEUS* (ca. 360 B.C.)

■ *This brings us to the question of whether women can properly be thought of as human.*

All that is distinctly human is the male. The males are the race; the females are merely the sex told off to reproduce it.
—GRANT ALLEN, *THE EVOLUTIONIST AT LARGE* (1881)

A woman is not a person as a chicken is not a bird.
—RUSSIAN PROVERB

Who thinks of a woman as a human being, a man inhabiting the moon, a goat as an animal, or a juniper as a tree?
—ESTONIAN PROVERB

The souls of women are so small
That some believe they have none at all.
—SAMUEL BUTLER, "MISCELLANEOUS THOUGHTS" (1605–10)

Women have no souls. They are super-aware slaves whose duties are to whelp and to serve men.
—CHARLES MANSON, AMERICAN MASS MURDERER (1968)

If you are not a man, you are nothing but a nonentity.
—BERNARR MACFADDEN, *THE VIRILE POWERS OF SUPERB MANHOOD* (1900)

Women are worthless wares.
—PERIPLECTOMENUS IN PLAUTUS, *MILES GLORIOSUS* (ca. 200 B.C.)

. . . the very gizzard of a trifle, the product of a quarter of a cipher, the epitome of nothing, fitter to be kicked if she were of a kickable substance, than either honor'd or humor'd.
—NATHANIEL WARD, *THE SIMPLE COBBLER OF AGGAWAM* (1646)

■ *So what function do women serve?*

Mistresses we keep for pleasure, concubines for daily attendance upon our persons, wives to bear us legitimate children and to be our faithful housekeepers.
—DEMOSTHENES, *ORATIONS* (ca. 340 B.C.)

Wives are young men's mistresses, companions for middle age, and old men's nurses.
—SIR FRANCIS BACON, "OF MARRIAGE AND THE SINGLE LIFE" (1625)

Woman is made for man. Man is made for life.
—RICHARD BURTON, BRITISH ACTOR (1975)

God made the woman for the use of man, and for the good and increase of the world.
—ALFRED, LORD TENNYSON, "EDWIN MORRIS" (1851)

Your women are a field for you to cultivate,
So go to your field as you will.
—MOHAMMAD, KORAN 2:223 (A.D. 624)

Her Lesser Biology

Here our patriarchs meet the challenge of reconciling the female's obvious insignificance in the cosmic scheme with her apparent importance in human reproduction. In this chapter the learned doctors, philosophers, and theologians will also debate the implications of woman's biological deformity (i.e., her lack of a penis): whether such a defective creature should have been made at all, and whether, in light of her deficiency, she can be considered, like man, to be made in the Image of God.

First, an analysis of her generative role.

Women have been created for the sake of propagation, the wife being the field, and the husband the giver of the seed. . . . Of the two parents, the father has greater authority, because the seed is superior to the womb.

—NARADA, *THE SACRED LAWS* (HINDU SCRIPTURE, 4TH CENTURY A.D.)

Woman furnishes the soil in which the seed of man finds the conditions required for its development. She nourishes and matures the seed without furnishing any seed herself. Thus man is never derived from woman, but always from man.

—PARACELSUS, *MAN AND THE CREATED WORLD* (1530)

The mother is no parent of that which is called her child, but only nurse of the new-planted seed that grows.

—APOLLO IN AESCHYLUS, *THE EUMENIDES* (458 B.C.)

The female is, as it were, an impotent male, for it is through a certain incapacity that the female is female, being incapable of concocting the nutriment [menstrual fluid] into semen because of the coldness of her nature. . . .

What the male contributes to generation is the form, or principle of movement, while the female provides the body, or in other words the material. . . . If we regard, then, the male, as male, as active and causing movement, and the female, as female, as passive and being set in movement, we see that the thing which is formed is formed *from them* only in the sense in which a bed is formed from the carpenter and the wood, or a ball from the wax and the form.

—ARISTOTLE, *ON THE GENERATION OF ANIMALS* (4TH CENTURY B.C.)

■ *A scientific explication from the great English physician Sir William Harvey, discoverer of the circulation of the blood:*

[Since] the substance of the uterus, when ready to conceive, is very like the structure of the brain, why should we not suppose that the function of both is similar. . . . And just as a "desire" arises from a conception of the brain, and this conception springs from some external object of desire, so also from the male, as being the more perfect animal, and, as it were, the most natural object of desire, does the natural [organic] conception arise in the uterus, even as the animal conception does in the brain. . . . From this desire, or conception, it results that the female produces an offspring like the father. . . . The "idea" or "form" of the father existing in the uterus generates an offspring like himself.

—SIR WILLIAM HARVEY, "ON CONCEPTION" (1651)

■ *What, then, is the origin of the human female?*

There is a good principle which created order, light, and man, and an evil principle which created chaos, darkness, and woman.
—PYTHAGORAS (6TH CENTURY B.C.)

Everything comes from God except women.
—ITALIAN PROVERB

Woman is originally an agent of the six devils and has been born as a woman to prevent man from following the way of the Buddha.
—ANON., *TAISETSU KYŌKUN ONNA SHIKIMOKU* (JAPANESE, 1745)

Women were created from the sediment of the sins of demons, to serve as temptation to sinners. . . . They are of value only as vehicles for the entry into the world of spirits condemned to take on temporary flesh as punishment for their sins . . . women themselves, however, being without soul.
—*OMM-AL-KITAB* (SCRIPTURE OF THE SHI'ITE SECT OF ISLAM)

Of those who were born as men, all that were cowardly and spent their life in wrongdoing were transformed at the second birth into women. . . . Such is the origin of women and of all that is female.
—PLATO, *TIMAEUS* (ca. 360 B.C.)

And the Lord God said, It is not good that the man should be alone; I will make him an help meet for him. . . .

And the Lord God caused a deep sleep to fall upon Adam, and he slept; and he took one of his ribs, and closed up the flesh instead thereof; and the rib, which the Lord God had taken from man, made he a woman, and brought her unto the man.

And Adam said, This is now bone of my bones, and flesh of my flesh: she shall be called Woman, because she was taken out of Man.

—OLD TESTAMENT, GENESIS 2:18–23 (ca. 700 B.C.)

■ *Why, one wonders, do some become female and others male?*

They who are full of sin beget only daughters.

—HINDU PROVERB

Men produce female as well as male seed. So do women. Male seed is stronger than female seed. . . . This is what happens: if the stronger seed comes from both sides, it produces a male; if the weaker, it produces a female. . . . Thus if the weaker seed is more abundant, the stronger is overcome, and, mingling with the weaker, is transformed and becomes female. But if the stronger is more abundant, then the weaker is overcome and becomes male.

—HIPPOCRATES, ON GENERATION (ca. 400 B.C.)

■ *To comprehend this generative principle, one must grasp the logic of the nature of female coldness.*

The female is more imperfect than the male. The first reason is that she is colder. If, among animals, the warmer ones are more active, it follows that the colder ones must be more imperfect. . . .

Just as man is the most perfect of all animals, so also, within the human species, man is more perfect than woman. The cause of this superiority is the [male's] superabundance of warmth, heat being the primary instrument of nature. . . .

The male's testicles are all the stronger because he is warmer. The sperm born there, on reaching the final degree of concoction, is the formative principle of the animal. From a single principle wisely imagined by the Creator—that whereby the female is less perfect than the male—follow all the conditions useful for the generation of the animal: the impossibility for the female genitalia to emerge externally, the accumulation of a superfluity of useful nourishment, an imperfect sperm, a hollow organ capable of receiving perfect sperm. In the male, instead, everything is the reverse: an elongated member suitable for copulation and emitting sperm, and an abundance of this same thick warm sperm.

—GALEN, *OF THE SEMEN* (2ND CENTURY A.D.)

■ *Aristotle continues his discussion from page 32 above:*

Why is it that one thing becomes and is male, and another female?

. . . Just as the young of mutilated parents are sometimes born mutilated and sometimes not, so also the young born of a female are sometimes female and sometimes male instead. For the female is, as it were, a mutilated male, and the catamenia [menstrual fluids] are semen, only not pure; for there is only one thing they have not in them, the principle of soul. . . . While the body is from the female, it is the soul that is from the male. . . .

The male is distinguished by his capacity to concoct blood into semen . . . and all concoction works by means of heat. Therefore the males of animals must needs be hotter than the females. For it is by reason of cold and incapacity that the female is more abundant in blood in certain parts of her anatomy. . . .

It will perhaps now be clearer for what reason one embryo becomes female and another male. For when the first principle does not bear sway and cannot concoct the nourishment through lack of heat nor bring it into its proper form, but is defeated in this respect, then must needs the material it works on change into its opposite. . . .

In human beings, the female fœtus is not perfected equally with the male. . . . For females are weaker and colder in nature, and we must look upon the female character as being a sort of natural deficiency. Accordingly while it is within the mother it develops slowly because of its coldness . . . but after birth it quickly arrives at maturity and old age on account of its weakness, for all inferior things come sooner to their perfection or end, and as this is true of works of art so it is of what is formed by nature.

—ARISTOTLE, *ON THE GENERATION OF ANIMALS* (4TH CENTURY B.C.)

■ *Others, too, have commented on girls' unseemly precocity.*

Girls begin to talk and to stand on their feet sooner than boys because weeds always grow up more quickly than good crops.

—MARTIN LUTHER, *TABLE TALK* (1533)

The nobler and more perfect a thing is, the later and slower it is in arriving at maturity. A man reaches the maturity of his reasoning powers and mental faculties hardly before the age of twenty-eight; a

woman, at eighteen. And then, too, in the case of woman, it is only reason of a sort—very niggardly in its dimensions. That is why women remain children their whole life long, never seeing anything but what is quite close to them, cleaving to the present moment, taking appearance for reality, and preferring trifles to matters of the first importance.
—ARTHUR SCHOPENHAUER, "ON WOMEN" (1851)

■ *Even tiny brains can perceive the evidence of their own inadequacy. Dr. Freud's seminal "penis envy" theory:*

The first step in the phallic phase . . . [is] a momentous discovery which little girls are destined to make. They notice the penis of a brother or playmate, strikingly visible and of large proportions, at once recognize it as the superior counterpart of their own small and inconspicuous organ, and from that time forward fall a victim to envy for the penis. . . .

[By contrast,] when a little boy first catches sight of a girl's genital region, he begins by showing irresolution and lack of interest. . . . It is not until later, when some threat of castration has obtained a hold upon him, that the observation becomes important to him . . . and forces him to believe in the reality of the threat which he has hitherto laughed at. This combination of circumstances leads to two reactions, which may . . . permanently determine the boy's relations to women: horror of the mutilated creature or triumphant contempt for her. . . .

A little girl develops differently. She makes her judgment and her decision in a flash. She has seen it and knows that she is without it and wants to have it.

From this point there branches off what has been named the masculinity complex of women. . . . The hope of some day obtaining a penis in spite of everything and so of becoming like a man may persist to an incredibly late age and may become a motive for the strangest and otherwise unaccountable actions. . . . Thus a girl may refuse to accept the fact of being castrated . . . and may subsequently be compelled to behave as though she were a man.

The psychical consequences of penis-envy . . . are various and far-reaching. After a woman has become aware of the wound to her narcissism, she develops, like a scar, a sense of inferiority. When she has passed beyond her first attempt at explaining her lack of a penis as being a punishment personal to herself and has realized that that sexual character is a universal one, she begins to share the contempt felt by men for a sex which is the lesser in so important a respect.

—SIGMUND FREUD, "SOME PSYCHICAL CONSEQUENCES OF THE ANATOMICAL
DISTINCTION BETWEEN THE SEXES" (1925)

■ *(For more of Dr. Freud's impressive theory, please see pages 86 and 215 below.)*

Every woman would prefer to be a man, just as every deformed wretch would prefer to be whole and fair, and every idiot and fool would prefer to be learned and wise.

—TORQUATO TASSO, AMINTA (1573)

There never lived a woman who did not wish she were a man. There never lived a man who wished he were a woman.

—E. W. HOWE, COUNTRY TOWNE SAYINGS (1911)

It is better to be a male for one day than a female for ten.

—KURDISH PROVERB

I thank thee, O Lord, that thou hast not created me a heathen . . . a slave . . . or a woman.

—ORTHODOX JEWISH DAILY MORNING PRAYER

■ *We can only ask, along with the poet:*

. . . Oh! why did God,
Creator wise, that peopl'd highest Heav'n
With Spirits Masculine, create at last
This noveltie on Earth, this fair defect
of Nature, [Woman] . . . ?

—JOHN MILTON, *PARADISE LOST* (1665)

■ *St. Thomas Aquinas (ca.* A.D. *1225–75), in his monumental* Summa Theologica, *confronts this crucial question.*

Question XCII, The Production of Woman

FIRST ARTICLE: Whether woman should have been made in the first production of things?

Objection 1. It would seem that woman should not have been made in the first production of things. For the Philosopher [Aristotle] says that *the female is a misbegotten male.* But nothing misbegotten or defective should have been made in the first production of things. Therefore woman should not have been made at that first production.

Objection 2. Further, subjection and limitation were a result of sin, for to the woman it was said after sin *Thou shalt be under the man's power* [Genesis 3:16]. . . . But woman is naturally of less strength and dignity than man. . . . Therefore woman should not have been made in the first production of things before sin.

Objection 3. Further, occasions of sin should be cut off. But God foresaw that woman would be an occasion of sin to man. Therefore He should not have made woman.

On the contrary, it is written [Genesis 2:18]: *It is not good for man to be alone; let us make him a helper like unto himself.*

I answer that, it was necessary for woman to be made, as the Scripture says, as a *helper* to man; not, indeed, as a helpmate in other works, as some say, since man can be more efficiently helped by another man in other works; but as a helper in the work of generation. . . . Among perfect animals, the active power of generation belongs to the male sex, and the passive power to the female. . . . But man is further ordered to a still nobler work of life, and that is intellectual operation. Therefore there was greater reason for the distinction of these two powers in man; so that the female should be produced separately from the male, and yet that they should be carnally united for generation.

—ST. THOMAS AQUINAS, *SUMMA THEOLOGICA* (1266–73)

■ *To put it more simply:*

I would have you know, that the head of every man is Christ, and the head of the woman is the man; and the head of Christ is God. . . . A man ought not to cover his head, inasmuch as he is the image and glory of God; but woman is the glory of man.

For man was not made from woman, but woman from man. Neither was man made for woman, but woman for man. That is why a woman ought to wear a veil on her head, because of the angels.
—NEW TESTAMENT, 1 CORINTHIANS 11:3–10 (ca. A.D. 50)

Do you know why God created women? Because sheep can't type.
—KENNETH ARMBRISTER, TEXAS STATE SENATOR (1989)

Man is the whole World and the Breath of God; Woman the Rib and crooked piece of Man.

—SIR THOMAS BROWNE, *RELIGIO MEDICI* (1642)

Man can attain direct experience of God; woman can attain it only through the man. Therefore every woman should treat her husband as God.

—YOGI BHAJAN, SIKH LEADER (1974)

No woman ought to be encouraged in the belief that she has separate interests or separate duties [from those of her husband]. God and Nature have merged her existence in that of her husband.

—EDITORIAL, *THE SATURDAY REVIEW* (1857)

■ *English Common Law, still observed in most of North America, continues to follow the sacred principles:*

By marriage, the husband and wife are one person in law; that is, the very being or legal existence of the woman is suspended during the marriage. . . .

—SIR WILLIAM BLACKSTONE, *COMMENTARIES ON THE LAWS OF ENGLAND* (1765)

Unclean and Disgusting

Life's primal transformations—the processes of birth and death, the mystery of blood—fill primitive Man with anxiety as well as awe. To help him cope with these uncomfortable sensations, rational Man enforces taboos to distance himself from the life processes and the women who embody them.

The dedicated misogynist must constantly remind himself that women are disgusting.

Every woman should be filled with shame by the thought that she is a woman.

—ST. CLEMENT OF ALEXANDRIA, *THE TUTOR* (ca. A.D. 190)

Woman is a temple built upon a sewer.

—BOETHIUS, *THE CONSOLATION OF PHILOSOPHY* (ca. A.D. 500)

Woman is nature, hence detestable.

—CHARLES BAUDELAIRE, *LES FLEURS DU MAL* (1857)

How can he be clean that is born of woman?

—OLD TESTAMENT, JOB 25:4 (ca. 325 B.C.)

You are inextricably involved with matter (i.e., mother), and moreover it is a sticky, messy, oozing business which makes you vomit.

—JEAN PAUL SARTRE, *NAUSEA* (1938)

The most holy bishop of Mainz was irritated by no annoyance more than by the stinking, putrid private parts of women.

—CROTUS RUBIANUS (ca. 1520)

. . . that unmentionable womb, that spongy pool, that time machine with a curse, dam for an ongoing river of blood.

—NORMAN MAILER, *THE PRISONER OF SEX* (1971)

I tend to regard the feminine organ as something unclean or as a wound . . . dangerous in itself, like everything bloody, mucous, infected.

—MICHEL LEIRIS, *AGE D'HOMME* (1946)

Dreams, myths, and cults attest to the fact that the vagina has and retains (for both sexes) connotations of a devouring mouth and an eliminating sphincter, in addition to being a bleeding wound.

—ERIK H. ERIKSON, "WOMANKIND AND THE INNER SPACE" (1968)

In conformity with the orthodox [Jewish] strictures, the sexual act is never performed in the light, nor is it permissible to look at the sexual organs of a woman.

—JEROME R. MINTZ, *LEGENDS OF THE HASIDIM* (1965)

How should we desire to embrace what is no more than a sack of dung!

—ST. ODO OF CLUNY (10TH CENTURY)

Once she'd sucked the marrow from my bones
And I turned to her for a languorous kiss,
Beside me I saw nothing more
Than a gluey-sided wineskin full of pus!

—CHARLES BAUDELAIRE, *LES FLEURS DU MAL* (1857)

Who except one bereft of sense would approve sensual pleasure itself, which is illicit, wallows in filthiness, is something that men censure, and that God without doubt condemns?

—SIR JOHN OF SALISBURY, BISHOP OF CHARTRES, "THE ANNOYANCE AND BURDENS OF WEDLOCK" (1159)

■ *From a scripture of the Jain religion:*

Infatuation, aversion, fear, disgust and various kinds of deceit [*māyā*] are ineradicable from the minds of women; for women, therefore, there is no nirvana. Nor is their body a proper covering; therefore they have to wear a covering. In the womb, between the breasts, in their navel and loins, a subtle emanation of life is continually taking place. How then can they be fit for self-control? A woman may be pure in faith and even preoccupied with the study of the sutras or the practice of a terrific asceticism: in her case there will still be no falling away of karmic matter.

—MAHAVIRA, *TĀTPARYA-VRITTI* (SCRIPTURE OF THE JAIN RELIGION, ca. 550 B.C.)

"There you have women," put in M. de Renal, with a coarse laugh. "There's always something wrong with their machinery."

—STENDHAL, *LE ROUGE ET LE NOIR* (1831)

You know women—there's always something bothering them.

—TOM JONES, WELSH ENTERTAINER (1977)

La femme est une maladie.

—JULES MICHELET, FRENCH HISTORIAN AND SCIENTIST, *L'AMOUR* (1897)

It's being sick makes them act so bloody awful usually and it's because they're sick you can't treat them as you should. The first great gift for a man is to be healthy and the second, maybe greater, is to fall [in] with healthy women. You can always trade one healthy woman in on another. But start with a sick woman and see where you get. Sick in the head or sick anywhere. But sick anywhere and in a little while they are sick in the head. If they locked up all the women who were crazy —but why speculate. . . . Anyway let's leave the subject. If you leave a woman, though, you probably ought to shoot her. It would save enough trouble in the end even if they hanged you.

—ERNEST HEMINGWAY, LETTER TO MAXWELL PERKINS (1943)

■ *The presumption is that women are perpetually unclean:*

Among the Gypsies . . . a woman was considered *marhime* [unclean] from the waist down and she must avoid letting the bottom of her skirts touch a man not her own, or anything he used. If her skirts should brush against plates, cups or drinking glasses, these were immediately destroyed, so as not to "soil" the next male user. . . .

A woman . . . should never pass in front of a man or between two men, but behind them; and if this was not possible, she should ask the men to turn away. . . . She should also at all times avoid passing in front of horses hitched onto a wagon.

—JAN YOORS, *THE GYPSIES* (1967)

Never wash in water that a woman has used . . . for there is a dismal forfeit that will contaminate [the male body].

—HESIOD, *WORKS AND DAYS* (ca. 800 B.C.)

■ *On esthetic grounds alone, the female has little to recommend her:*

The female body, even at its best, is very defective in form; it has harsh curves and very clumsily distributed masses; compared to it the average milk-jug, or even cuspidor, is a thing of intelligent and gratifying design. . . . Below the neck by the bow and below the waist astern there are two masses that simply refuse to fit into a balanced composition. Viewed from the side, a woman presents an exaggerated *S* bisected by an imperfect straight line, and so she inevitably suggests a drunken dollar-mark.

—H. L. MENCKEN, "IN DEFENSE OF WOMEN" (1918)

■ *A sampling of medical information about the female anatomy:*

Nature has placed in the female body, in a secret and intestinal place, a certain animal or member which is not in man, in which are engendered, frequently, certain humours, brackish, nitrous, voracious, acrid, mordant, shooting, and bitterly tickling.

—RONDIBILIS IN FRANÇOIS RABELAIS, M.D., *PANTAGRUEL* (1533)

On the whole, the womb is like an animal within an animal. . . . [It] also is subject to the affections of an animal in smelling; for it follows after fragrant things as if for pleasure, and flees from fetid and disagreeable things as if for dislike.

—ARETAEUS OF CAPPADOCIA, PHYSICIAN (ca. A.D. 100)

The menstrual blood escapes by the feeblest parts of the body, in the same way that wine or beer undergoing fermentation escapes by defective parts of the barrel.

—REGNIER DE GRAAF, M.D., *ON THE FEMALE TESTES OR OVARIES* (ca. 1670)

Contact [with menstrual blood] turns new wine sour, crops touched by it become barren, grafts die, seed in gardens are dried up, the fruit of trees falls off, the edge of steel and the gleam of ivory are dulled, hives of bees die, even bronze and iron are at once seized by rust, and a horrible smell fills the air; to taste it drives dogs mad and infects their bites with an incurable poison.

—PLINY THE ELDER, *NATURAL HISTORY* (A.D. 77)

■ *Some primitive beliefs about menstruation:*

Contact with menstrual blood or a menstruating woman will sicken a man and cause persistent vomiting, kill his blood so that it turns black, corrupt his vital juices so that his skin darkens and hangs in folds as his flesh wastes, permanently dull his wits, and eventually lead to a slow decline and death.

—THE MAE ENGA OF NEW GUINEA (20TH CENTURY)

During their menstrual periods, [aboriginal] Australian women are forbidden under pain of death to touch anything that men use, or even to walk on a path that men frequent. They are also secluded at childbirth, and all vessels then used by them are burned. In Uganda, pots which a woman touches while the impurity of menstruation is upon her have to be destroyed; spears and shields defiled by her touch are, however, merely purified. No Exquimaux of Alaska will willingly drink out of the same cup or eat out of the same dish that has been used by a woman at her confinement until it has been purified by certain incantations. Among some of the Indians of North America women at menstruation are forbidden to touch men's utensils, which would be so defiled by their touch that their subsequent use would be attended by certain mischief or misfortune. Among the Bribri Indians of Costa Rica a menstruous woman is regarded as unclean. The only plates she may use for her food are banana leaves, which, when she has done with them, she throws away in some sequestered spot; for were a cow to find them and eat them, it would waste away. And she drinks out of a special vessel for a like reason: if any one drank out of the same cup after her, he would surely die.

—SIR JAMES GEORGE FRAZER, *THE GOLDEN BOUGH* (1890)

■ *More sophisticated patriarchs have incorporated these beliefs into law:*

And if a woman have an issue, and her issue in her flesh be blood, she shall be put apart seven days: and whosoever toucheth her shall be unclean until the even.

And every thing that she lieth upon in her separation shall be unclean: every thing also that she sitteth upon shall be unclean. And whosoever toucheth her bed shall wash his clothes, and bathe himself in water, and be unclean until the even. And whosoever toucheth any thing that she sat upon shall wash his clothes, and bathe himself in water, and be unclean until the even. . . .

And if any man lie with her at all, and her flowers be upon him, he shall be unclean seven days; and all the bed whereon he lieth shall be unclean.

—OLD TESTAMENT, LEVITICUS 15:19–24 (6TH CENTURY B.C.)

According to the Laws of Manu, "The wisdom, the energy, the strength, the right, and the vitality of a man who approaches a menstruous woman, utterly perish." In short, the attitude of man, and not only savage man to a menstruating woman, is well expressed in the rhyme:

Oh! menstruating woman, thou'rt a fiend

From whom all nature should be closely screened.

—ERNEST CRAWLEY, THE MYSTIC ROSE (1902)

■ *According to the Parsi religion:*

Hands sprinkled in ceremonial abolution, when a menstruous woman sees them, become quite unclean by her look, and even if she looks hastily, and does not see, the sacred twigs, it is the same. . . . Prepared food which is within three steps of a menstruous woman is polluted by her. . . .

And the sun and other luminaries are not to be looked at by her, and animals and plants are not to be looked at by her, and conversation with a righteous man is not to be held by her; for a fiend so violent is the fiend of menstruation, that, where another fiend does not smite anything with a look, it smites with a look. . . .

And during her menstruation she is to be so situated that, from her body, there are fifteen steps of three feet to water, fifteen steps to fire, fifteen steps to the sacred twigs, and three steps to a righteous man. And her food is to be carried forth in iron or leaden vessels; and the person who shall carry forth the food stands at three steps away from her. . . .

That which comes from a menstruous woman to any one, or to any thing, is all to be washed in bull's urine and water.

—ZEND-AVESTA, SHAYAST-LA-SHAYAST (6TH CENTURY A.D.)

■ *How, then, can any rational man entertain the illusion called* **love?** *What, in fact,* **is** *love? For an expert and inspired opinion, let us turn to Count Donatien Alphonse François, Marquis de Sade (worshiped by the Romantics as "the Divine Marquis"). From his immortal* **Juliette** *(1798):*

Love is nothing but a perverse superstition found amongst some few decadent peoples; the majority of the world's societies that wisely keep their women under lock and key to minimize their mischief never succumb to this particular mental disease. If we trace the superstition back to its source we will have no difficulty in either proving it a disease or recognizing the remedy.

Our so-called chivalry, which consists in absurdly venerating an object intended to serve our needs, derives from the fear of witches that once plagued our ignorant ancestors. Their terror was transmuted, first into respect, then into worship; thus gallantry was miraculously born from the womb of ignorant superstition. But such respect is fundamentally unnatural, since Nature nowhere gives a single instance of it. *The natural inferiority of women* to men is universally evident, and nothing intrinsic to the female sex naturally inspires respect. . . .

Wherever men live in harmony with Nature they invariably hold women in the profoundest contempt. . . . If we are to deify an object simply because it has some utility, let us bow down as well to our bulls, our mules, and our chamberpots. . . .

Such is the scorn for women among the Croats . . . that when referring to their wives they employ exactly the same vocabulary and tone they use when referring to other beasts of burden. Croatian women sleep on the bare ground, they do as they are ordered instantly and without a whisper of protest, and they are thrashed mercilessly at the least hint of recalcitrance. Their subjection and drudgery are never lifted, even during pregnancy . . . and Croatian children are said to be the healthiest and strongest, and Croatian wives the most faithful, of any in the world. Thus does Nature reward those who treat females as they obviously deserve to be treated.

In the Zaporarian Cossack country women are excluded from the clan. Those whose services are required for propagation are allowed to live, but are kept isolated on islands, where the men visit them whenever they feel the need, using them haphazardly and indifferently, without regard for age, appearance, or kinship. . . .

In many parts of the world menstruating women are treated like beasts. They are kept in cages, or tied to stakes, and food is thrown to them from a distance, as one feeds bears or tigers. Do you suppose such peoples are much plagued by this business of "falling in love"?

In the African kingdom of Louango pregnant women are treated even more harshly. They are considered to be even more than normally

polluted, deformed and disgusting; and indeed, what is more repugnant to the eye than an expectant mother? Pregnant and naked: thus should women be exhibited to their admirers; for these clearly have a taste for the hideous and the grotesque. . . .

The ancient Romans and Celts held life and death power over their women, and exercised it frequently. Nature obviously intended Man to have this right, as attested by his superior physical strength. When we deprive men of this right, we mock Nature's laws.

Female bondage is near-absolute throughout most of Africa; a woman feels herself honored if her husband condescends to climb her.

The odious sex is so miserably mistreated in Juida that women recruited for the harems of the prince frequently commit suicide; for that august sovereign never uses a woman without punishing her horribly afterward for having incited his lust.

Turning to Asia, we find there proud despots whose . . . enviable delight is in collecting girls of the utmost purity and most delicate beauty, and subjecting them to the most hideous and bestial indulgences the informed imagination can conceive. Thus righteously do they reduce to the basest degradation those insolent divinities whom we, to our eternal disgrace, revere.

The Chinese have the loftiest contempt for women, and consider them barely fit to be diddled, and even less fit to be seen. . . .

Believe me, gentlemen, it was not to see us grovel in the grip of a sentiment so demeaning as love that Nature placed muscle and brains on the side of the male. Not at all! We were so endowed in order to rule that feeble and deceitful sex, to force them into the service of our desires. We deny Nature's most manifest intent when we accord any independence, let alone ascendancy, to those inferior beings whom Nature clearly created to be our slaves.

. . . Promiscuity and copious copulation! These are the best antidotes to love. . . . Let a man indulge himself regularly with a variety of females, and his heart will lose the insidious softness that renders it susceptible to love's delusion. Sexually satiated, the heart grows tough, and the patient is cured.

. . . Every experienced man knows that the woman trying hardest to trap him is concealing defects which would rapidly disgust him if he only knew what they were. The appropriate exercise here is to imagine those defects, probe the ugly possibilities, envision every revolting detail. If one practices this meditation whenever he feels himself in danger of "falling in love," the fire may be extinguished before it goes out of control.

Is she a girl? Then she somewhere exudes some vile odor. If she does not now, she will later. So why run panting after a cesspool?

Is she a woman? Another man's leavings may, I admit, momentarily rouse desire. But *love*? Tell me, what can there be to idolize? If not already, she soon will be, a vast vat for brewing brats. Just picture emerging from that cavity you covet a shapeless mass of flesh, sticky and squirming. . . .

Mentally undress this idol of your soul. . . . Is it over those two bent and stubby thighs that you're ready to spout poetry? Or over that fetid and fathomless gulf where they meet? Or perhaps it's this untidy apron of dirty, matted hairs hanging between those same slovenly thighs that fires your imagination! Or is it, perhaps, those two flaccid hunks of meat drooping flabbily against her navel? No? Then doubtless it's on the far, not the near, side that you find what inflames your folly. Voilà! Behold those two sagging wattles of tired, wax-colored flesh, sheltering that puckered little brown mouth whence emerge her turds. Yes, these are the glories that inspire you to rhapsodies, and for whose sake you are willing to sink into a condition lower than that of a worm.

But wait, you say, I have misunderstood. It is not any of this but her "finer qualities" that enchant you. I see. By this you mean, no doubt, her cunning, conniving character, her relentless treachery, her ceaselessly wagging, nagging tongue, her inane vanity, her meows and purrs and hissings, her whorishness and prudery (for Woman spends her entire life vacillating between these two extremes). Or perhaps you have in mind her spitefulness, her obstinacy, her mindless illogic, her caviling, cawing stupidity. Yes, doubtless these are the "finer qualities" you find to revere in the object of your affections. . . .

If I may be permitted a scientific digression, I would like to call to your attention the fact that the difference between man and woman is approximately the same as that between man and ape. Therefore we should no more include women in the human species than we should consider a baboon our brother. . . . It is mainly in her failings that the human female differs from other animals; thus we may well assert that she is inferior to them. . . .

To understand the extent to which reason may be unhinged by metaphysical frenzy, listen to some love-befuddled nitwit declare that it is not his beloved's body he wants, but her heart. Her heart?! The very object that should inspire in him only horror and revulsion. Where is the precedent for such an extravagant perversion?

But—I anticipate your objection—hasn't this same type of worship always existed? For instance, the Greeks and Romans deified Love and His mother. This is true. . . . However, in discussing objects of worship, one does not always help one's case by calling upon the ancients. People who worshiped excrement under the name of the god Stercutius, and adored sewers in the form of the goddess Cloacina, might very understandably have worshiped women, since their odor bears a close enough resemblance to the two aforementioned divinities.

—COUNT DE BELMOR IN MARQUIS DE SADE, *JULIETTE* (1798)

Women are here to serve men. Look at them, they got to squat to piss. Hell, that proves it.

—LARRY FLYNT, AMERICAN PUBLISHER (1976)

Insatiable as the Grave

Man experiences the ultimate terror, annihilation, every time a woman receives his virility. Orgasm has been called "the little death" since time immemorial.

If sex resembles death, then woman resembles the grave: ravenous, dark, obscene.

Many woes, strange and dire,
Many terrors earth has bred;
. . . Of the hurricane wrath
Of winds, too, marvels might be told.
But . . . none may tell
Of how passion's wild, reckless power,
Fraught with human ruin,
Rules o'er woman's stubborn mind.
When perverse rebellious love
Masters the feminine heart,
Then destroyed is the union
Of mated lives for beast or man.

—CHORUS IN AESCHYLUS, *CHOEPHORAE* (458 B.C.)

The strange woman's mouth is a deep pit;
He whom the Lord hates shall fall into it.

—OLD TESTAMENT, PROVERBS 22:14 (ca. 900 B.C.)

. . . the strange woman, she the flower, the sword
Red from spilt blood, a mortal flower to men,
Adorable, detestable . . .
> —ALGERNON CHARLES SWINBURNE, *ATALANTA IN CALYDON* (1865)

■ *The fact is, all women are "strange": that is, predatory.*

Men, some to Business, some to Pleasure take;
But every Woman is at heart a Rake.
> —ALEXANDER POPE, "OF THE CHARACTERS OF WOMEN" (1732–33)

Long ago there lived a woman named Moârbeda, a noted philosopher who was reputed to be the wisest person of her time. It is recorded that one day some questions were put to her, and these were some of her replies:

"In what part of woman's body does her mind reside?"

"Between her thighs."

"And in what place does she experience her greatest pleasure?"

"The same."

"And what is a woman's religion?"

"Her vulva."

"And with what part of herself does she love and hate?"

"The same. . . . We give our vulva to the man we love and refuse it to the man we hate."
> —SHEIKH OMAR EN-NEFZAWI, *THE PERFUMED GARDEN* (ca. A.D. 500)

What then? Have not women this renewal of the mind in which is the image of God? Who would say this? But in the sex of their body they do not signify this; therefore they are bidden to be veiled. The part, namely, which they signify in the very fact of their being women, is that which may be called the concupiscential part.

—ST. AUGUSTINE, *OF THE WORKS OF MONKS* (ca. A.D. 400)

Indeed, the whole of the woman's body is to be regarded as pudental and no part of her may lawfully be seen by anyone but her husband or close kin, except in case of need (as when she is undergoing medical treatment).

—AL-BAYDAWI, PERSIAN KORANIC SCHOLAR (13TH CENTURY)

By "woman" is meant sensuality itself, which is well signified by woman, since in woman this naturally prevails.

—PETER LOMBARD, *SENTENTIAE* (1155)

Most women have small waists the
   world throughout,
But their desires are a thousand
   miles about.

—AMBITOSO IN CYRIL TOURNEUR, *THE REVENGER'S TRAGEDY* (1607)

Every woman loves more than a man does, but out of shame she hides the sting of love, although she be mad for it.

—NONNUS, *DIONYSIACA* (ca. A.D.500)

■ *Women are constantly thinking about sex:*

The greater part of women, whatever it be that they see, do always represent unto their fancies, think and imagine, that it hath some relation to the sugared entering of the goodly ithyphallos. . . .

—RONDIBILIS IN FRANÇOIS RABELAIS, *PANTAGRUEL* (1533)

■ *Is there such a thing as a chaste woman?*

She is chaste who was never asked the question.

—ENGLISH, FRENCH, GREEK, AND LATIN PROVERBS

In the absence of men all women are chaste.

—SANSKRIT PROVERB

No is no negative in a woman's mouth.

—SIR PHILIP SIDNEY, *THE COUNTESS OF PEMBROKES ARCADIA* (1580)

There is no female so modest that she will not be stirred with passion at the advances of a stranger.

—SIR JOHN OF SALISBURY, BISHOP OF CHARTRES,
"THE ANNOYANCE AND BURDENS OF WEDLOCK" (1159)

It may be possible to find some women who have never had an affair of the heart, but it would be rare to find any who have had only one.

—FRANÇOIS, DUC DE LA ROCHEFOUCAULD, *MAXIMES* (1665).

Girls are for the most part confirmed in all the hateful arts of coquetry, and attend with *gusto* rather than with distaste, the hideous desires and terrible satisfactions of men.

—AUBREY BEARDSLEY, *UNDER THE HILL* (1903)

Upon a headstrong daughter keep strict watch,
   Lest, finding liberty, she use it for herself.
Watch over an impudent eye,
   And marvel not if she trespass against thee.
She will open her mouth like a thirsty traveler,
   And drink of every water that is near;
By every hedge will she sit down,
   And open her quiver against every arrow.

—APOCRYPHA, ECCLESIASTICUS 26:10–12 (ca. 200 B.C.)

■ *Even married women suffer from a hellish lust:*

Women that are of good family, beautiful, and well married do not stay within the moral bounds. This is the failing in women. . . . There is not a man they would not go to—be he old or young, handsome or ugly—for they think to themselves only: "He is a man," and want to enjoy him. . . . Even those women who are held in high esteem, watched over and loved, they too, given the chance, will fasten even onto hunchbacks, the blind, simpletons, dwarfs, and cripples. . . . And when women cannot come on to a man at all, they even fall lustfully on one another, for they will never be true to their husbands. . . .

The fire has never too many logs, the great sea never too many rivers, death has never too many beings of all kinds, and lovely-eyed woman has never too many men. This, O divine Rishi, is the secret of all women. So soon as a woman sees a handsome man, her vulva

becomes moist. . . . Not the richest enjoyment of their wishes, not ornaments, not protection and home do they hold in such esteem as satisfaction and pleasure in love.

The god of death, the wind, the underworld, the ever-burning entrance to hell, the knife-edge, poison, serpent, and fire—women are all of these in one.

Ever since the five elements have been, and the worlds have been made, ever since men and women were made—ever since then, these faults have been in women.

—A SAGE IN *THE RÂMÂYANA* (ca. 500 B.C.)

Need makes the old wife trot.

—ENGLISH PROVERB (13TH CENTURY)

Water, fire and women will never say, "Enough!"

—POLISH AND SWISS PROVERBS

When a woman's lips say, "It is enough," she looks at you with her eyes and they say, "Again."

—CHINESE PROVERB

Aside from ejaculation, there are two major areas of physiologic difference between female and male orgasmic expression. First, the female is capable of rapid return to orgasm immediately following an orgasmic experience, if restimulated before tensions have dropped below plateau-phase response levels. Second, the female is capable of maintaining an orgasmic experience for a relatively long period of time.

—W. H. MASTERS AND V. E. JOHNSON, *HUMAN SEXUAL RESPONSE* (1966)

Of women's unnatural, unsatiable lust, what country, what village doth not complain?

—ROBERT BURTON, *THE ANATOMY OF MELANCHOLY* (1621)

■ *Most offensive of all, women love love more than they love men.*

Women for the most part do not love us. They do not choose a man because they love him, but because it pleases them to be loved by him. They love love of all things in the world, but there are very few men whom they love personally.

—ALPHONSE KARR, *LES GUÊPES* (1839)

In their first passions women are in love with their lover; in all the rest, with love.

—FRANÇOIS, DUC DE LA ROCHEFOUCAULD, *MAXIMES* (1665)

■ *Women's affection for men (if any) is random and indiscriminate:*

A woman's heart, like the moon, is always changing, but there is always a man in it.

—ANON., *PUNCH* (ca. 1920)

Women have one man in their heart, another in their words, and still another in their arms.

—MAHAVIRA, *PRAVACANA-SARA* (SCRIPTURE OF THE JAIN RELIGION, ca. 550 B.C.)

A woman talks to one man, looks at a second, and thinks of a third.

—BHARTRIHARI, *SRINGA SATAKA* (BUDDHIST SCRIPTURE, ca. A.D. 625)

■ *They are all the same:*

There's only one thing worse than a shameless woman,
And that's another woman!

—CHORUS IN ARISTOPHANES, *THE THESMOPHORIAZUSAE* (411 B.C.)

■ *How foolish of women to behave unchastely, thereby devaluing themselves!*

Ah, wasteful woman, she who may
    On her sweet self set her own price,
Knowing man cannot choose but pay,
    How has she cheapen'd paradise;
How given for nought her priceless gift,
    How spoil'd the bread and spill'd the wine,
Which, spent with due, respective thrift,
    Had made brutes men, and men divine.

—COVENTRY PATMORE, *THE ANGEL IN THE HOUSE* (1854)

■ *Some classical warnings:*

Men, hear my words about Woman!
Her lust is writ between her eyes.
Heed not her words, though she be the Sultan's daughter;
Her malice is infinite. . . .
Men, beware and belay the love of Woman!
Never say "I love you"
Or "This is my companion."
She loves you only while you're thrusting—
That kind of love can not last.
Lying on her breast, you love her. . . .
Fool! In the morning she'll call you a pig!
And this too is something nobody questions:
Wives entertain slaves in the husband's bed.
Trust a woman and lose your head!
—SHEIKH OMAR EN-NEFZAWI, *THE PERFUMED GARDEN* (ca. A.D. 500)

Rely not on women, trust not in their hearts;
Their faith is found in their private parts.
—ABU-NUWĀS (ca. A.D. 800)

Who trusts a woman, that man trusts a swindler.
—HESIOD, *WORKS AND DAYS* (ca. 800 B.C.)

Do not trust the winter sun or a woman's heart.
—BULGARIAN PROVERB

The vows that a woman makes to her lover
Are only fit to be written on air.
—CATULLUS, *CARMINA* (ca. 60 B.C.)

If thou givest thy heart to a woman she will kill thee.

—KANURI PROVERB (NORTHERN NIGERIA AND THE SUDAN)

■ *Woman destroys man's spirit as well as his body:*

A woman blossoms for us precisely at the right moment to plunge a man into everlasting ruin; such is her natural destiny.

—ALVA IN FRANK WEDEKIND, *PANDORA'S BOX* (1904)

Woman's love is a devil's net.

—SERBO-CROATIAN PROVERB

You'd take to bed the whole world as your prize,
you slut of sluts, by boredom brutalized. . . .
O blind and deaf machine, rich in torment—
drinker of the world's blood, wholesome instrument,
how can you not feel shame . . .
that nature, strong in her concealed designs
makes use of you, o woman, queen of sins,
vile animal! to mould a genius?
O foul magnificence—sublime disgrace!

—CHARLES BAUDELAIRE, *LES FLEURS DU MAL* (1857)

Politics are a woman. If you are her unfortunate lover, she will bite
your head off.

—ADOLF HITLER (ca. 1935)

■ *"the escape"*:

escape from the black widow spider
is a miracle as great as art.
what a web she can weave
slowly drawing you to her
she'll embrace you
then when she's satisfied
she'll kill you
still in her embrace
and suck the blood from you.

I escaped my black widow
because she had too many males
in her web
and while she was embracing one
and then the other and then
another
I worked free
got out
to where I was before.

she'll miss me—
not my love
but the taste of my blood,
but she's good, she'll find other
blood;
she's so good that I almost miss my death,
but not quite;
I've escaped. I view the other
webs.

—CHARLES BUKOWSKI, "THE ESCAPE" (1977)

For all Christ's work this Venus is not quelled,
But reddens at the mouth with blood of men,
Sucking between small teeth the sap o' the veins,
Dabbling with death her little tender lips—
A bitter beauty, poisonous-pearled mouth. . . .
. . . men must always love you in life's spite;
For you will always kill them; man by man
Your lips will bite them dead; yea, though you would,
You shall not spare one; all will die of you. . . .
. . . Ah, fair love,
Fair fearful Venus made of deadly foam,
I shall escape you somehow with my death.

—ALGERNON CHARLES SWINBURNE, *CHASTELARD* (1865)

■ *Even death is preferable to sexual engagement with women.*

Better fall into the fierce tiger's mouth, or under the sharp knife of the executioner, than to dwell with a woman and excite in yourselves lustful thoughts.

Better far with red-hot pins bore out both your eyes, than encourage in yourselves lustful thoughts, or look upon a woman's form with such desires.

—BUDDHA (ca. 500 B.C.), IN *A LIFE OF BUDDHA* (BUDDHIST SCRIPTURE, ca. A.D. 100)

A stain upon our chastity is accounted by us more dreadful than any punishment of any death . . . therefore is woman the obstacle to purity, the temptress, the enemy . . . her body is the gate of hell.

—TERTULLIAN, *APOLOGETICUS* (ca. A.D. 200)

The obscenity of the feminine sex is that of everything which "gapes open." It is an *appeal to being* as all holes are. In herself woman appeals to a strange flesh which is to transform her into a fullness of being by penetration and dissolution. . . . Beyond any doubt her sex is a mouth and a voracious mouth which devours the penis—a fact which can easily lead to the idea of castration. The amorous act is the castration of the man; but this is above all because sex is a hole.

—JEAN PAUL SARTRE, *BEING AND NOTHINGNESS* (1943)

■ *Both science and folk wisdom bear this out.*

A lively and passionate woman can severely damage a man, causing impotence.

—EMIL PETERS, M.D., *DIE WIEDERGEBURT DER KRAFT* (1908)

The vagina is very hot, it is fire and each time the penis goes in it dies.

—A CENTRAL AUSTRALIAN MAN, TO GÉZA RÓHEIM (1935)

That which destroys man is the vulva.

—A MAORI ELDER, TO GÉZA RÓHEIM (1935)

O woman, woman, woman, woman!
. . . Torturous as Hell, insatiate as the grave.

—SCUDMORE IN NATHANIEL FIELD, *A WOMAN IS A WEATHERCOCK* (1612)

Evil Is Woman

Given that woman is alien, inferior, unclean, and ravenous, her moral character is no mystery.

More bitter than death I find woman,
Whose heart is like nets and snares,
And whose hands are like brazen bands.
Who pleases the Lord shall escape her,
But the sinner will fall in her trap.
Lo, this have I found, says the Preacher,
Adding up one by one,
Which still my soul seeks but can not find:
I have found one good man in a thousand,
But not one good woman among them.

—OLD TESTAMENT, ECCLESIASTES 7:26–28 (ca. 400 B.C.)

A virtuous woman! Nay, I swear
By good St. Denis, that's more rare
Than is a phoenix.

—GUILLAUME DE LORRIS, *ROMAN DE LA ROSE* (13TH CENTURY)

A man is as good as he has to be,
and a woman as bad as she dares.

—ELBERT HUBBARD, *THE PHILISTINE* (1900)

. . . He seldom errs
Who thinks the worst he can of womankind.

—GLENALVON IN JOHN HOME, DOUGLAS (1756)

Beautiful woman, beautiful trouble.

—JAMAICAN PROVERB

■ *Even women have no use for women.*

Women are sisters nowhere.

—WEST AFRICAN PROVERB

One woman never praises another.

—ESTONIAN PROVERB

Did any woman ever acknowledge profundity in another woman's mind, or justice in another woman's heart?

—FRIEDRICH NIETZSCHE, BEYOND GOOD AND EVIL (1886)

However bad the things a man may think about women, there is no woman who does not think worse of them than he.

—SÉBASTIAN NICOLAS CHAMFORT, MAXIMES (1794)

■ *The problem is that women lack proper values.*

There are only three things in the world that women do not understand; and they are Liberty, Equality and Fraternity.

—G. K. CHESTERTON, "WOMEN" (1910)

Women will avoid the wicked not because it is unright, but only because it is ugly. . . . Nothing of duty, nothing of compulsion, nothing of obligation! . . . They do something only because it pleases them. . . . I hardly believe that the fair sex is capable of principles.

—IMMANUEL KANT, *OBSERVATIONS ON THE FEELING OF THE BEAUTIFUL AND THE SUBLIME* (1764)

No lady was ever a gentleman.

—GERALD IN JAMES BRANCH CABELL, *SOMETHING ABOUT EVE* (1927)

■ *This is because badness is part of the fundamental nature of women.*

Women, so helpless in doing good deeds,
Are of every evil the cleverest contrivers.

—MEDEA IN EURIPIDES, *THE MEDEA* (431 B.C.)

Women, at best, are bad.

—BELLAFONT IN THOMAS DEKKER, *THE HONEST WHORE* (1604)

Women are like herrings: when good, they are only middling; and when bad, they are bad.

—CORNISH PROVERB

Oh the gladness of her gladness when she's glad,
And the sadness of her sadness when she's sad;
   But the gladness of her gladness,
   And the sadness of her sadness,
   Are as nothing, Charles,
To the badness of her badness when she's bad.

—SIR JAMES M. BARRIE, *ROSALIND* (ca. 1900)

■ *. . . At least, compared to men.*

Better the badness of men than the goodness of women.
—APOCRYPHA, ECCLESIASTICUS 42:14 (ca. 200 B.C.)

For men at most differ as Heaven and Earth,
But women, worst and best, as Heaven and Hell.
—ALFRED, LORD TENNYSON, *IDYLLS OF THE KING* (1859)

■ *Looking on the bright side:*

When a woman is openly bad, then at least she is honest.
—LATIN PROVERB

There are many good women, but they are all dead.
—GERMAN AND SPANISH PROVERBS

■ *This is why our discerning patriarchs trace all of humanity's troubles back to women.*

In all the woes that curse our race
There is a lady in the case.
—W. S. GILBERT, "FALLEN FAIRIES" (ca. 1866)

There was never a conflict without a woman.
—ALBANIAN PROVERB

Clearly all disasters, or an enormous proportion of them, are due to the dissoluteness of women.
—LEO TOLSTOY, *DIARY* (DECEMBER 19, 1900)

There is not a war in the world, no, nor an injustice, but you women are answerable for it.

—JOHN RUSKIN, *SESAME AND LILIES* (1865)

. . . There's no motion
That tends to vice in man, but I affirm
It is the Woman's part: be it Lying, note it,
The woman's; Flattering, hers; Deceiving, hers;
Lust and rank thoughts, hers; Revenges, hers;
Ambitions, Covetings, change of Prides, Disdain,
Nice longings, Slanders, Mutability,
All faults that may be named, nay, that hell knows,
Why, hers, in part or all; but rather, all;
For even to vice
They are not constant, but are changing still
One vice, but of a minute old, for one
Not half so old as that.

— LEONATUS POSTHUMUS IN WILLIAM SHAKESPEARE, *CYMBELINE* (1610)

■ *The evil of women may be thought of as a sort of natural calamity.*

It is nature's law that rivers wind, trees grow wood, and, given the opportunity, women work iniquity.

— TRIPITAKA, *SUTTA-PITAKA* (BUDDHIST SCRIPTURE, ca. A.D. 50)

From the sea, much salt; from women, much evil.

— SPANISH PROVERB

Of all the plagues with which the world is curst,
Of every ill, a woman is the worst.

— AMADIS IN GEORGE GRANVILLE, *THE BRITISH ENCHANTERS* (ca. 1700)

Of all the wild beasts on land or sea, the wildest of all is woman.

— MENANDER, *E SUPPOSITITIO* (ca. 300 B.C.)

Her dove-like eyes turn'd to coals of fire,
  Her beautiful nose to a terrible snout,
Her hands to paws, with nasty great claws,
  And her bosom went in and her tail came out.
—RICHARD HARRIS BARHAM, "A LAY OF ST. NICHOLAS" (1837)

Women are one and all a set of vultures.
—GAIUS PETRONIUS, SATYRICON (1ST CENTURY A.D.)

There is no such poison in the green snake's mouth, or the hornet's sting, as in a woman's heart.
—CHINESE PROVERB

Nature doth paint them further to be weak, frail, impatient, feeble and foolish; and experience hath declared them to be unconstant, variable, cruel, and lacking the spirit of counsel.
—JOHN KNOX, THE FIRST BLAST OF THE TRUMPET AGAINST THE MONSTROUS REGIMENT OF WOMEN (1560)

Woman would be more charming if one could fall into her arms without falling into her hands.
—AMBROSE BIERCE, EPIGRAMS (1911)

Woman is the emissary of hell; she destroys the seed of Buddha. Her face resembles that of a saint; her heart is like that of a demon.
—ANON., TAISETSU KYŌKUN ONNA SHIKIMOKU (JAPANESE, 1745)

■ *Everyone agrees that women are fundamentally diabolical:*

Woman is man's Satan.
—ARABIC, DANISH, GERMAN, GREEK, HINDU, MALAYAN, PERSIAN, POLISH, AND RUSSIAN PROVERBS

O woman, woman, when to ill thy mind
Is bent, all hell contains no fouler fiend.

—AGAMEMNON IN HOMER, *ODYSSEY* (ca. 800 B.C.)

When toward the Devil's house we tread,
Woman's a thousand steps ahead.

—MEPHISTOPHELES IN JOHANN WOLFGANG VON GOETHE, *FAUST* (1808)

Mom is everywhere and everything and damned near everybody. . . .
Disguised as good old mom, dear old mom, sweet old mom, your
loving mom, and so on, she is the bride at every funeral and the corpse
at every wedding.

—PHILIP WYLIE, *A GENERATION OF VIPERS* (1942)

But the Woman that God gave him, every fibre of her frame
Proves her launched for one sole issue, armed and engined for the same;
And to serve that single issue, lest the generations fail,
The female of the species must be deadlier than the male.

—RUDYARD KIPLING, "THE FEMALE OF THE SPECIES" (1892)

Don't you think that robbing a corpse is indicative of a mean, petty
and womanish spirit?

—SOCRATES IN PLATO, *THE REPUBLIC* (ca. 380 B.C.)

■ *Let us look specifically at the evils peculiar to women. First, her*
guile.

Lo! the guile of women is very great.

—MOHAMMAD, KORAN 12:28 (A.D. 620)

O the unsounded sea of women's bloods,
That when 'tis calmest, is most dangerous! . . .
Not Cerberus ever saw the damned nooks
Hid with the veils of women's virtuous looks.
—MONSIEUR IN GEORGE CHAPMAN, *BUSSY D'AMBOIS* (1607)

A strange woman's lips with honey drip,
    And her mouth is smoother than oil;
But her end is as bitter as wormwood,
    As sharp as a two-edged sword.
—OLD TESTAMENT, PROVERBS 5:3–4 (ca. 900 B.C.)

The whole world is strewn with snares, traps, gins and pitfalls for the capture of men by women.
—GEORGE BERNARD SHAW, *MAN AND SUPERMAN* (1903)

The ingenuity of a guileless woman will undermine nine mountains.
—CHINESE PROVERB

■ *Next, her sadism.*

The tactics of woman seem not only predatory and primitive, but monstrous; because she is conscious of her weakness she destroys what is weak. Woman is the great abortionist. Woman plunders, castrates, dishonors, destroys. In contrast to masculine sadism woman's sadism is chronic, lasting, and unappeasable. Limited in her psychic development by her strict biologic functioning, woman in her abnormal behavior betrays a cruelty which seems quixotic and paradoxical, but which upon analysis, is seen to be inevitable and in accordance with her nature. After coition she enchains man and treats him like a child;

instead of employing contraceptives she resorts to abortive methods; after procreation she enslaves her children and maintains them in a condition of absolute dependence. . . . In the fulfillment of her sadistic urges the tactics of woman resemble more the terrifying and monstrous practices met with in the insect world.

—DR. R. ALLENDY, "SADISM IN WOMEN" (1933)

Women delight in administering the birch; and innumerable are the tales of schoolmistresses whipping their pupils, mothers, and especially mothers-in-law, their children, and taking grim pleasure in the operation. Indeed women are more cruel and relentless than men.

—HENRY SPENCER ASHBEE, *INDEX LIBRORUM PROHIBITORUM* (1877)

Then, my boy, beware of Daphne.
   Learn a lesson from the rat:
What is cunning in the kitten
   May be cruel in the cat.

—ROBERT UNDERWOOD JOHNSON, "DAPHNE" (ca. 1910)

■ *Her vengefulness.*

Revenge is when a woman gets even with a man for what she's done to him.

—AMERICAN JOKE (ca. 1960)

Sweet is revenge—especially to women.

—LORD BYRON, *DON JUAN* (1818)

. . . Revenge, we find,
Ever the pleasure of a petty mind,
And hence so dear to poor weak womankind.

—JUVENAL, *SATIRES* (ca. A.D. 100)

In revenge as in love woman is always more barbarous than man.
—FRIEDRICH NIETZSCHE, *BEYOND GOOD AND EVIL* (1886)

Women and elephants never forget an injury.
—REGINALD IN H. H. MUNRO (SAKI), "REGINALD" (1904)

■ *Her jealousy.*

Heaven has no rage like love to hatred turned,
Nor hell a fury like a woman scorned.
— ZARA IN WILLIAM CONGREVE, *THE MOURNING BRIDE* (1697)

Jealousy is inborn in women's hearts.
— CHORUS IN EURIPIDES, *ANDROMACHE* (ca. 420 B.C.)

The venom clamours of a jealous woman
Poisons more deadly than a mad dog's tooth.
— ABBESS IN WILLIAM SHAKESPEARE, *THE COMEDY OF ERRORS* (1592–93)

You may take it as an instance of male injustice if I assert that envy and jealousy play an even greater part in the mental life of women than of men.
— SIGMUND FREUD, "FEMININITY" (1933)

■ *Dr. Freud's remarkable "penis envy" theory, continuing from page 38 above, here explains women's moral and ethical deficiencies:*

Even after penis-envy has abandoned its true object, it continues to exist: by an easy displacement it persists in the character-trait of *jealousy*. Of course, jealousy is not limited to one sex . . . but I am of the opinion that it plays a far larger part in the mental life of women than of men and that that is because it is enormously reinforced from the direction of a displaced penis-envy. . . .

I cannot escape the notion (though I hesitate to give it expression) that for women the level of what is ethically normal is different from what it is in men. . . . Character-traits which critics of every epoch have brought up against women—that they show less sense of justice than men, that they are less ready to submit to the great necessities of life, that they are more often influenced in their judgments by feelings of affection or hostility—all these would be amply accounted for by the modification in the formation of their super-ego which we have already inferred. We must not allow ourselves to be deflected from such conclusions by the denials of the feminists, who are anxious to force us to regard the two sexes as completely equal in position and worth.

—SIGMUND FREUD, "SOME PSYCHICAL CONSEQUENCES OF THE ANATOMICAL DISTINCTION BETWEEN THE SEXES" (1925)

Whoever called women the fair sex didn't know anything about justice.

—AMERICAN JOKE (ca. 1965)

■ *Many profound thinkers agree that so-called emancipated women are the worst offenders against God and Man.*

Feminists and all these radical gals—most of them are failures. They've blown it. Some of them have been married, but they married some Casper Milquetoast who asked permission to go to the bathroom. These women just need a man in the house. That's all they need. Most of these feminists need a man to tell them what time of day it is and to lead them home. And they blew it and they're mad at all men. Feminists hate men. They're sexist. . . . That's their problem.

—REV. JERRY FALWELL (1989)

I don't like the women's liberation movement. I think that it's harmful for women to become immersed in politics. It's just another way for women to imitate men, and women will wind up being hurt by it. . . .

I don't know why the women's liberation movement dislikes me so. Women have been a definite influence on my life. I adore women as a whole. I enjoy them as a breed, like a dog. They're another species that you become endeared to. I don't mean that derogatorily, but in an admiring sense, like someone would appreciate a fine breed of horse. It's like treading on eggs not to offend these people, the women's libbers. They're touchy, always on the defensive. What are they so worried about?

—HENRY MILLER, INTERVIEW (1975)

The only alliance I would make with the Women's Liberation Movement is in bed.

—ABBIE HOFFMAN, AMERICAN POLITICAL REVOLUTIONARY (1972)

Women's libbers are a pain in the ass. I treat women the way I always did, except I treat women's libbers different: if I catch one, I try and screw her a little harder.

There're still plenty of women around, thank Christ, who are happy to be a part of the life of a good man, and who'll take care of their end of it. A woman's place is in the bedroom and in the kitchen and taking care of her kids. . . . You find one that's happy, she won't be out looking for a job.

—EVEL KNIEVEL, AMERICAN DAREDEVIL, INTERVIEW (1978)

One who admits publicly to be a member of an organization that promotes abortions, such as the National Organization for Women, must be refused the Sacrament of the Eucharist by priests, deacons and extraordinary ministers. Nor can they proclaim the word of God by serving as lector, for they ignore God's law and His love.

—LEO T. MAHER, BISHOP OF SAN DIEGO, "LETTER ON ABORTION" (APRIL 1, 1975)

Emancipated Woman, trampling under foot the laws of God in nature and revelation, so far from being a purifying and refining element in society, is herself an incarnate demon, with nothing womanly in her but the name, a creature of unbounded lust and merciless cruelty, a combination of Messalina and Lady Macbeth.

—REV. PETER Z. EASTON, *DOES WOMAN REPRESENT GOD?* (ca. 1890)

■ *This brings us to a question of burning importance to churchmen over the centuries: Why is the abominable crime of witchcraft so much more prevalent among women than among men?*

All authorities on witchcraft have made it clear that for every male witch there are fifty female witches. . . . This is the case not because

of their frailty (since most of them are incorrigibly obstinate), but because of their bestial cupidity. . . . And this is very likely why Plato placed women between man and the brute beasts [*Timaeus,* 91a–c]. For it is obvious that woman's visceral parts are larger than those of man, whose cupidity is less violent. At the same time, men have larger

heads, and therefore more brains and sense, than women. The ancient poets were expressing this metaphorically when they said that Pallas Athena, the goddess of wisdom, was born directly from the brain of Jupiter and had no mother: thus they indicated that wisdom never comes from woman, whose nature more resembles that of the brute beasts. We note that Satan first approached the woman, who then seduced the man. For it was God's plan to humble Satan by giving him power generally and primarily over the least worthy creatures, such as snakes and vermin and other beasts that God's law calls foul; and next over other beasts rather than over men; and then over woman rather than man. . . . Thus Satan makes use of wives in order to ensnare their husbands.

—JEAN BODIN, ON THE DEMON-WORSHIP OF SORCERERS (1580)

My marriage taught me many lessons, and this not the least: when women are devoted to children—a few rare individuals are capable of other interests—they take a morbid pleasure in conspiring against a husband, especially if he be a father. They take advantage of his pre-occupation with his work in the world to conceive and execute every kind of criminally cunning abomination. The belief in witchcraft was not all superstition; its psychological roots were sound. Women who are thwarted in their natural instincts turn inevitably to all kinds of malignant mischief, from slander to domestic destruction.

—ALEISTER CROWLEY, THE SPIRIT OF SOLITUDE (1929)

■ *The* Malleus Maleficarum, *or* Hammer of Witches *(1486), was the official handbook for judges whose task it was to submit suspected witches to the Inquisition. The book remained continuously in print for two hundred years, going to twenty-nine editions between 1487 and 1660.*

Why Superstition is Chiefly Found in Women

As to why a greater number of witches is found in the fragile feminine sex than among men, it is indeed a fact that it were idle to contradict, since it is accredited by actual experience, apart from the verbal testimony of credible witnesses. . . .

The first [reason] is, that they are more credulous; and since the chief aim of the devil is to corrupt faith, therefore he rather attacks them. . . . The second reason is that women are naturally more impressionable, and more ready to receive the influence of a disembodied spirit. . . . The third reason is that they have slippery tongues, and are unable to conceal from their fellow women those things which by evil arts they know; and, since they are weak, they find an easy and secret manner of vindicating themselves by witchcraft. . . .

For as regards intellect, or the understanding of spiritual things, they seem to be of a different nature from men; a fact which is vouched for by the logic of the authorities. . . .

But the natural reason is that she is more carnal than a man, as is clear from her many carnal abominations. And it should be noted that there was a defect in the formation of the first woman, since she was formed from a bent rib. . . . And since through this defect she is an imperfect animal, she always deceives. . . . Wherefore it is no wonder that so great a number of witches exist in this sex. . . .

If we inquire, we find that nearly all the kingdoms of the world have been overthrown by women. Troy . . . was, for the rape of one woman, Helen, destroyed, and many thousands of Greeks slain. The kingdom of the Jews suffered much misfortune and destruction through the accursed Jezebel. . . . The kingdom of the Romans endured much evil through Cleopatra . . . that worst of women. And so with others. Therefore it is no wonder if the world now suffers through the malice of women. . . . Justly may we say with Cato of Uitca: If the world could be rid of women, we should not be without God. . . .

To conclude. All witchcraft comes from carnal lust, which is in women insatiable. . . . Wherefore for the sake of fulfilling their lusts they consort even with devils. . . . And blessed be the Highest Who has so far preserved the male sex from so great a crime: for since He was willing to be born and to suffer for us, therefore He has granted to men this privilege.

—JAMES SPRENGER AND HEINRICH KRAMER, *MALLEUS MALEFICARUM* (1486)

■ *Perhaps not all women are witches, but feminine evil is surely the worst of the world's ills.*

Give me any disease but a plague of the heart,
  And any evil but that of a woman. . . .
No poison is deadly as that of a serpent;
  No wrath is wilder than that of a woman.
I'd live in a den with a lion and a dragon
  Before I'd keep house with a wicked woman.
A woman's wickedness blackens her look
  And darkens her face so she looks like a bear.
In the midst of his friends her husband sits,
  And blind to the world, he bitterly sighs:
All malice is nothing to that of a woman,
  May the lot of the wicked fall on her! . . .
A humbled heart and a sorrowful face
  And a heart-wound, is an evil wife:
A woman who will not comfort her man
  Weakens his hands and enfeebles his knees.
Of woman came the beginning of sin,
  And thanks to her, we all must die.
Give not to water an outlet,
  Nor to a wicked woman power:
If she does not go just as you want her to,
  Chase her from your bed,
  Give her a divorce,
  And let her go.

—APOCRYPHA, ECCLESIASTICUS 25:13–26 (ca. 200 B.C.)

The Wise Man
Will Avoid Them

In light of the evidence presented above, it is clear that the most prudent course to take with respect to women is to avoid them altogether.

The way to fight a woman is with your hat—grab it and run.
—JOHN BARRYMORE, AMERICAN ACTOR (ca. 1925)

Regard the society of women as a necessary unpleasantness of social life, and avoid it as much as possible.
—LEO TOLSTOY, *DIARY* (JUNE 16, 1847)

Best a pint of wine and keep away from women.
—SWISS PROVERB

The desirable things in life are: first, whiskey; second, tobacco; third, horses; fourth, guns; fifth, women.
—ARAPAHO INDIANS (1835)

It is better to be without a wife for a year than without tobacco for an hour.
—ESTONIAN PROVERB

A woman is only a woman, but a good Cigar is a smoke.
—RUDYARD KIPLING, "THE BETROTHED" (1885)

The world is full of care, like unto a bubble,
Women and care, and care and women,
    and women and care and trouble.

—NATHANIEL WARD, *THE SIMPLE COBBLER OF AGGAWAM* (1646)

■ *Some practical advice:*

"How are we to conduct ourselves, Lord, with regard to woman-kind?"

"Don't see them, Ânanda."

"But if we should see them, what are we to do?"

"Abstain from speech, Ânanda."

"But if they should speak to us, Lord, what are we to do?"

"Keep wide awake, Ânanda."

—BUDDHA (ca. 500 B.C.), IN *THE BOOK OF THE GREAT DECEASE*
(BUDDHIST SCRIPTURE, ca. 300 B.C.)

O race of mankind, beware the honeysweet poison,
And seductive song and the lure of that fearful chasm,
O fear the raging flames of that furious dragon!
—BISHOP MARBOD DE RENNES (ca. 1105)

■ *Joseph Swetnam's lavish* **Arraignment of Lewde, Idle, Fro-ward, and Unconstant Women** *(1615) remained continuously in print for more than two hundred years:*

The Lyon being bitten with hungre, the Beare being robbed of her young ones, the Viper being trod on, all these are nothing so terrible as the fury of a woman. A bucke may be inclosed in a Parke, a bridle rules a horse, a Woolfe may be tyed, a Tyger may be tamed, but a froward woman will never be tamed, no spur will make hir goe, nor no bridle will holde hir backe, for if a woman holde an opinion no man can draw hir from it, tell hir of hir fault she will not beleeve that she is in any fault, give hir good counsell but she will not take it, if you doe but looke after another woman then she will be jealous, the more thou lovest hir the more she will disdaine thee, and if thou threaten hir then she will be angry, flatter hir and then she will be proude . . . : what wise man then will exchange golde for drosse, pleasure for paine, a quiet life for wrangling braules, from the which the married men are never free. . . .

Yet there are many young men which cudgell their witts and beate theire braines and spend all their time in the love of women, and if they get a smile or but a favor at their loves hand, they straight way are so ravished with joy, yea so much they thinke they have gotten God by the hand, but within a while after they will find that they have the Devill by the foote. . . .

And what of all this? why nothing but to tell thee that a woman is better lost than found, better forsaken than taken.

. . . A gentleman on a time said to his friend I can helpe you to a good marriage for your sonne, his friend made him this answer: my sonne (said hee) shall stay till he have more wit: the Gentleman replied againe, saying, if you marrie him not before he hath wit, he will never marry so long as he liveth.

For a married man is like unto one arrested. . . . [And] if thou marriest onely for bare love, then thou wilt afterwards with sorrow say that there is more belonges to housekeeping then fower bare legges in a bed. . . . To what end then should we live in love, seeing it is a life more to be feared than death, for all thy monie wastes in toyes and is spent in banquetting, and all thy time in sighs and sobbs to thinke upon thy trouble and charge which commonly commeth with a wife. . . .

What wilt thou that I say more oh thou poore married man. . . . A woman which is faire in showe is foule in condition, she is like unto a glowworme which is bright in the hedge and black in the hand; in the greenest grasse lyeth hid the greatest Serpents: painted pottes commonly holde deadly poyson: and in the clearest water the ugliest Tode, and the fairest woman hath some filthiness in hir.

—JOSEPH SWETNAM, *THE ARRAIGNMENT OF LEWDE, IDLE, FROWARD,*
AND UNCONSTANT WOMEN (1615)

. . . And what are these vermin
of Hell itself but women? . . .
    As flees the seagull
from the quick-winged eagle,
as lambs from the wolf bound
or fawn from slim-hipped hound,
so a poor wretch fears
the witchery of these dears,
their flattery and their tears.
    Tears of a crocodile,
hyena ways of guile;

when a monstrous woman vile
greets you with a winning smile
she'll lead you to a mazy toil.
   . . . Never in my life
have I heard of strife
end in mastery of a wife.

        —HOMER BRYDYDD, "AGAINST WOMEN, A SATIRE" (WELSH, ca. 1550)

It is my duty, gentlemen, to inform you that women are dictators all,
and I recommend to you this moral:
In real life it takes only one to make a quarrel.

        —OGDEN NASH, MARRIAGE LINES (1964)

■ *The perils of matrimonial life cannot be overstated.*

The man who is either ensnared by the charms of a wife, or induced
by natural affection to make his children his first care, is no longer the
same towards others, but has unconsciously become changed from a
free man into a slave.

        —PHILO JUDAEUS (ca. A.D. 30)

He that hath wife and children hath given hostages to fortune; for they
are impediments to great enterprises, either of virtue or of mischief
. . . He was reputed one of the wise men, that made answer to the
question, when a man should marry: "A young man not yet, an elder
man not at all."

        —SIR FRANCIS BACON, "OF MARRIAGE AND THE SINGLE LIFE" (1625)

Art thou young? Then match not yet; if old, match not at all.

        —GREEK PROVERB (5TH CENTURY A.D.)

A young man married is a man that's marred.

        —PAROLLES (THE FOOL) IN WILLIAM SHAKESPEARE, ALL'S WELL THAT ENDS WELL (1602)

Every woman should marry—and no man.
—HUGO BOHUN IN BENJAMIN DISRAELI, *LOTHAIR* (1870)

If men knew how women pass the time when they are alone, they'd never marry.
—YELLOW DOG IN O. HENRY, "MEMOIRS OF A YELLOW DOG" (ca. 1905)

Marriage is a custom brought about by women who then proceed to live off men and destroy them, completely enveloping the man in a destructive cocoon or eating him away like a poisonous fungus on a tree.
—RICHARD HARRIS, BRITISH ACTOR (1983)

Whoever saith that marriage is to be put above virginity or celibacy, and that it is not more blessed to remain chaste than to marry, let him be anathema.
—DECREE OF THE COUNCIL OF TRENT (1564)

■ *Proverbs advising men against matrimony constitute an abundant body of thought.*

The woman cries before the wedding and the man after.
—POLISH PROVERB

Whoso is tired of happy days let him take a wife.
—DUTCH PROVERB

A wedding lasts a day or two, but the misery forever.
—CZECH PROVERB

He that has a wife has a master.
—SCOTTISH PROVERB (18TH CENTURY)

Who hath a wife hath also an enemy.

—SPANISH PROVERB

If wives were good, God would have had one.

—GEORGIAN PROVERB

A married man is a caged bird.

—GENOESE PROVERB

Strife is the dowry of a wife.

—OVID, *AMORES* (ca. A.D. 15)

Bigamy is having one wife too many. Monogamy is the same.

—BRITISH JOKE (19TH CENTURY)

■ *Why men continue perversely to ignore the wisdom of the ages is one of life's great mysteries.*

Yet thou, they say, for marriage dost provide:
Is this an age to buckle with a bride? . . .
A sober man like thee to change his life!
What fury would possess thee with a wife!
Art thou of every other death bereft,
No knife, no ratsbane, no kind halter left?
(For every noose compared to hers is cheap)
Is there no city-bridge from whence to leap?
Wouldst thou become her drudge, who dost enjoy
A better sort of bedfellow, thy boy?
He keeps thee not awake with nightly brawls,
Nor with a begg'd reward thy pleasure palls;

Nor with insatiate heavings calls for more,
When all thy spirits were drain'd out before.
But still Ursidius courts the marriage bait,
Longs for a son to settle his estate. . . .
The man's grown mad: to ease his frantic pain,
Run for the surgeon; breathe the middle vein:
. . . And let him every deity adore,
If his new bride prove not an arrant whore
In head and tail, and every other pore.

—JUVENAL, *SATIRES* (ca. A.D. 100)

■ *The female's menace is inherent in her physiology.*

Being ensnared by the beauty of a lovely person, . . . thou knowest
not, poor wretch, that what thou seekest is a chimera. But thou art
doomed to know that this triform monster, although it is beautified
with the face of a noble lion, yet is blemished with the belly of a reeking
kid and is beweaponed with the virulent tail of a viper.

—WALTER MAP, "LETTER FROM VALERIUS TO RUFFINUS" (ca. 1200)

. . . In a year or less,
Or two at most, my lovely, lively bride
Is turned a hag, a fury by my side,
With hollow yellow teeth, or none perhaps,
With stinking breath, swart cheeks, and hanging chaps,
With wrinkled neck, and stooping as she goes,
With driveling mouth, and with a sniveling nose.

—GUILLAUME DE SALLUSTE, SEIGNEUR DU BARTAS, *DIVINE WEEKS* (ca. 1580)

Marriage is the best magician there is. In front of your eyes it can change an exciting, cute little dish into a boring dishwasher.

—RYAN O'NEAL, AMERICAN ACTOR (1978)

■ *But let us look on the bright side. The female's unfortunate suscep-*
tibility to aging provides her the opportunity to perform one final kind-
ness for her long-suffering husband.

Your wife is good when she forsakes this light
And yields by force to nature's destiny:
She better is, though living, if she die,
But best, the sooner she does take her flight;
For so to you your ease she does restore,
Which soonest had, will comfort you the more.

—FRANCIS THYNNE, "EPIGRAMS" (1600)

A woman gives a man but two happy days: the day he marries her, and the day he buries her.

—HIPPONAX OF EPHESUS (6TH CENTURY B.C.)

■ *Hipponax's witticism enjoyed currency for well over two thousand*
years.

A man is twice happy: when he marries a wife, and when he buries her.

—GREEK PROVERB (5TH CENTURY A.D.); SIMILARLY: MONTENEGRIN, RUSSIAN, SERBIAN,
AND YUGOSLAVIAN PROVERBS

Although all womankind be nought, yet two good days hath she:
Her marriage day, and day of death, when all she leaves to thee.
—TIMOTHY KENDALL, *FLOWER OF EPIGRAMS* (ca. 1650)

In every marriage two things are allowed,
A wife in wedding-sheets and in a shroud;
How can the marriage state then be accurst,
Since the last day's as happy as the first?

—ANON., *AGREEABLE COMPANION* (1745)

■ *But it would be unworthy of our patriarchs to limit dead-wife jokes to a single punch line.*

A dead wife under the table is the best goods in a man's house.

—JONATHAN SWIFT, *POLITE CONVERSATION* (1738)

Here lies my wife: here let her lie!
Now she's at rest, and so am I.

—JOHN DRYDEN, "SUGGESTED EPITAPH FOR HIS WIFE" (ca. 1675)

The lucky man loses his wife, the unlucky one his horse.

—GEORGIAN PROVERB

Both women and dragons are best out of the world.

—PERSIAN PROVERB

Henry VIII . . . didn't get divorced, he just had [his wives'] heads chopped off when he got tired of them. That's a good way to get rid of a woman—no alimony.

—TED TURNER, AMERICAN MEDIA MOGUL (1983)

A man named Pacuvius, bursting into tears, told his neighbor Arrius, "I have in my garden a barren tree on which my first wife hanged herself, and then my second, and just now my third."

Arrius answered, "I marvel that thou hast found cause for tears in such a run of good luck," and again, "Great heavens, what heavy costs to thee hang from that tree!" And thirdly, "My friend, give me of that tree some branches to plant."

—MEDIEVAL JESTS, RETOLD BY WALTER MAP, "LETTER FROM VALERIUS TO RUFFINUS"
(ca. 1200)

■ *Jesting aside, woman's fundamental threat is to Man's unique and precious spirituality.*

Were there no women, men might live as gods.

—CANDIDO IN THOMAS DEKKER, *THE HONEST WHORE* (1604)

They who spend much time with women cease to practice meditation.

—*SUTRA-KRIT-ANGA* (SCRIPTURE OF THE JAIN RELIGION, ca. 500 B.C.)

Nothing so much casts down the mind of man from its citadel as do the blandishments of women, and that physical contact without which a wife cannot be possessed.

—ST. AUGUSTINE, *SOLILOQUIES* (ca. A.D. 387)

So long as a man desires women his mind is in bondage, as a calf that drinks milk is in bondage to its mother.

—BUDDHIST PROVERB, FROM THE *DHAMMAPADA* (BUDDHIST SCRIPTURE, ca. A.D. 100)

Countless are woman's defects.
My elephantine mind has fallen
Into the poisonous swamp of guile.
So I must renounce the world.

—NĀROPA, TIBETAN MYSTIC POET (ca. A.D. 1050)

■ *Nāropa's austere conclusion has been shared by many, but not all aspiring ascetics find celibacy an easy path. Manuals for the edification of monks abound in cautionary tales.*

From a thirteenth-century guidebook for Cistercian novices:

Monk: "I will not tell of those who have consented to lechery and fallen, but of those who, tempted and shaken, have yet been preserved by God's grace.

"A certain rich and honourable knight, being separated from his wife according to Church custom, came to a house of our Order for the sake of conversion. To this monastery he gave all his possessions, on the condition that it should pay a certain life-pension to his wife, who had promised to lead a religious life in some nunnery. . . . When he had become a novice, the Devil so pricked her that she drew back from her purpose, and asked again for her husband, who was by now become a Brother of the house. Seeing then that she profited nothing by such means, . . . she kept silence for all that year; but after his year of probation, being driven by some necessity, he revisited his house with a monk for his companion, and there he found the lady aforesaid. She, making as though she would have spoken with him in private, led him to her chamber, closed the door privily, and began to embrace and to kiss him; hoping that, if she might lead him into sin, he would leave the Order and come back to her. But Christ the Son of spotlessness . . . saved also this knight of His from the unlawful embraces of his lawful spouse. For, shaking himself free from her arms, he went forth unhurt, and unsinged by the fire. . . .

Novice: "That was a great temptation!"

—CAESARIUS OF HEISTERBACH, *DIALOGUS MIRACULORUM* (ca. A.D. 1225)

■ *From a world away comes a virtually identical admonitory anecdote.*

In golden gear bedecked, a troop of maids
Attending in her train, bearing the babe
Upon her hip, my wife drew near to me.
I marked her coming, mother of my child,
In brave array, like snare of Māra laid.
Thereat arose in me the deeper thought:
Attention to the fact and to the cause.
The misery of it all was manifest;
Distaste, indifference, the mind possessed;
And so my heart was set at liberty.
O see the seemly order of the Norm!
The Threefold Wisdom have I made my own,
And all the Buddha bids me do is done.
　　　　　　　—TRIPITAKA, *SUTTA-PITAKA* (BUDDHIST SCRIPTURE, ca. 80 B.C.)

■ *Parallel tales:*
The Novice and the Geese

A young anchorite, who had been nourished from his childhood in the
hermitage, went with his abbot to the city; and, seeing women dancing
together, he enquired earnestly of his abbot what these might be.

"They are geese," quoth he.

When therefore the boy was come back to the cloister, he presently
fell a-weeping; to whom the abbott [said]: "What wouldst thou, my
son?"

"Father," quoth he, "I would fain eat of those geese which I saw in
the city."
　　　　　　　—ANON., *LATIN STORIES*, A COLLECTION OF
　　　　　　　13TH- AND 14TH-CENTURY PREACHERS' MANUALS

■ *The Novice and the Tigers*

A young monk, who had been raised from early childhood in the monastery, went one day with his teacher to the city. Seeing women for the first time, he asked his teacher what these might be.

"They are tigers," replied the teacher, "and they will eat you up."

Returning to the monastery, the boy seemed lost in thought. Finally he spoke. "If those are tigers, Reverend Sir," he said, "then I would prefer to be eaten."

—ANON., TRADITIONAL CHINESE TAOIST STORY

■ *Sympathetic to Man's evident weakness in this regard, our religious masters are not inflexible.*

It is good for a man not to touch a woman. . . . I say therefore to the unmarried and widows, It is good for them if they abide even as I. But if they cannot contain, let them marry: for it is better to marry than to burn.

—NEW TESTAMENT, 1 CORINTHIANS 7:1, 8–9 (ca. A.D. 50)

It is better to marry only because it is worse to burn. It is still better neither to marry nor to burn.

—TERTULLIAN, *AD UXOREM* (ca. A.D. 205)

Part Two

.

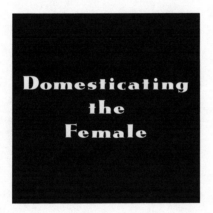

Domesticating
the
Female

FOR THOSE WHO ARE UNABLE TO AVOID WOMEN,
IT IS ESSENTIAL TO KNOW HOW TO CONTROL THEM.

The Law of Obedience

Considering the perversity of the female creature and her uncanny hold over men's minds, it is clear that the survival of patriarchal civilization itself, as well as the security of individual men, demands rigorous enforcement of male supremacy.

Over the years our patriarchs have evolved programs for the subjugation of women that have proved not only effective but also philosophically consistent, in that they accord impeccably with the theories devised to justify them.

First consider the Law of Nature.

It is the law of nature that woman should be held under the dominance of man.

—CONFUCIUS (ca. 500 B.C.)

Although there may be exceptions to the order of nature, the male is by nature fitter for command than the female, just as the elder and full-grown is superior to the younger and more immature. . . . The relation of the male to the female is of this kind, but there the inequality is permanent.

—ARISTOTLE, *POLITICS* (4TH CENTURY B.C.)

In the family, it is clear, for several reasons which lie in its very nature, that the father ought to command. In the first place, the authority ought not to be equally divided between father and mother; the government must be single, and in every division of opinion there must be one preponderant voice to decide. Secondly, however lightly we may regard the disadvantages peculiar to women, yet, as they necessarily occasion intervals of inaction, this is a sufficient reason for excluding them from this supreme authority: for when the balance is perfectly even, a straw is enough to turn the scale. Besides, the husband ought to be able to superintend his wife's conduct, because it is of importance for him to be assured that the children, whom he is obliged to acknowledge and maintain, belong to no one but himself.

—JEAN JACQUES ROUSSEAU, *A DISCOURSE ON POLITICAL ECONOMY* (1755)

■ *Anatomical differences ordain this Law.*

Indeed, according to the law that Nature gives them, it is not proper for them to will and desire; their role is to suffer, obey, consent. That

is why Nature has given them a perpetual capacity, to us a rare and uncertain one. They have their hour always, so that they may be ready for ours: *born to be passive* (Seneca). And whereas Nature has willed that our appetites should show and declare themselves prominently, she has made theirs occult and internal, and has furnished them with parts unsuitable for show and simply for the defensive.

—MONTAIGNE, MICHEL DE, ESSAYS (1588)

■ *Above all, it is practical considerations—the prevention of male confusion highest among them—that ordain the supremacy of Man.*

Man for the field and woman for the hearth:
Man for the sword and for the needle she:
Man with the head and woman with the heart:
Man to command and woman to obey:
All else confusion.

—ALFRED, LORD TENNYSON, "THE PRINCESS" (1847)

The husband and wife, though they have but one common concern, yet having different understandings, will unavoidably sometimes have different wills too. It therefore being necessary that the last determination (i.e., the rule) should be placed somewhere, it naturally falls to the man's share as the abler and the stronger.

—JOHN LOCKE, CONCERNING CIVIL GOVERNMENT (1690)

The emotion-nature (woman) must be subject to the dictates of the reasoning mind (man), or truth, justice, equity, peace, mercy, are suppressed in the soul.

—G. A. GASKELL, DICTIONARY OF ALL SCRIPTURES AND MYTHS (1960)

Therefore Gods universal Law
Gave to the man despotic power
Over his female in due awe. . . .
So shall he least confusion draw
On his whole life, not sway'd
By female usurpation, nor dismay'd.

—JOHN MILTON, *SAMSON AGONISTES* (1671)

■ *How convenient it is that God Himself ordained the subordination of women.*

Unto the woman [God] said, "I will greatly multiply thy sorrow and thy conception; in sorrow thou shalt bring forth children; and thy desire shall be to thy husband, and he shall rule over thee."

—OLD TESTAMENT, GENESIS 3:16 (ca. 900 B.C.)

Wives, submit yourselves unto your own husbands, as is fit in the Lord.

—NEW TESTAMENT, COLOSSIANS 3:18 (ca. A.D. 50)

Since *God* has determined subjection to be woman's lot, there needs no other argument of its fitness, or for their acquiescence. . . . A wife should be inquisitive only of new ways to please her husband, and should sayle her wit only by his compass, looking upon him as conjurers do the circle, beyond which there is nothing but Death and Hell.

—REV. RICHARD BRAITHWAITE (1633)

The Holy Scriptures show that it is clearly the will of God that man should be superior in power and authority to woman. . . . No lesson is more plainly and frequently taught in the Bible, than woman's subjection. . . . If the position assumed by the [suffragist] women be true, then must the Divine Word from Genesis to Revelation be set aside as untrue.

—REV. HENRY GREW, IN DEBATE AT THE
FIFTH NATIONAL WOMAN'S RIGHTS CONVENTION (1854)

■ *It is not only Western religions that prescribe absolute obedience for women. Oriental decrees, however, attribute the inevitability of female*

submission neither to pragmatism nor to the will of the Deity, but to qualities within the female herself.

Such is the stupidity of woman's character that it is incumbent upon her, in every particular, to distrust herself and to obey her husband.

—CONFUCIUS (ca. 500 B.C.)

The five worst infirmities that afflict the female are indocility, discontent, slander, jealousy, and silliness. It is from these that arises the inferiority of women to men.

—EKKEN KAIBARA, *GREATER LEARNING FOR WOMEN*
(TRADITIONAL JAPANESE MARRIAGE MANUAL, 15TH CENTURY)

Men are superior to women on account of the qualities in which God has given them pre-eminence, and because they spend of their property [for the support of women].

—MOHAMMAD, KORAN 4:34 (A.D. 626)

■ *The age or financial solvency of the woman in question is not the issue.*

It does not belong to a woman to determine anything of herself, but she is subject to the Rule of the Three Obediences. When she is young she has to obey her parents; when married she has to obey her husband; when a widow she has to obey her son.

—MENCIUS, CHINESE PHILOSOPHER (ca. 320 B.C.)

In childhood, a woman must be subject to her father; in youth, to her husband; when her husband is dead, to her sons. A woman must never be free of subjugation. . . .

Though destitute of virtue, or seeking pleasure elsewhere, or completely devoid of good qualities, a husband must be constantly worshipped as a god by the faithful wife.

—MANU, *THE SACRED LAWS* (HINDU SCRIPTURE, ca. 100 B.C.)

Man, but not woman, is made in the image of God. It is plain from this that women should be subject to their husbands, and should be as slaves.

—GRATIAN, *DECRETUM* (1140)

■ *The institution of slavery, as a matter of fact, provides the perfect model for the ideal relations between male and female.*

In the first place there must be a union of . . . male and female, that the race may continue . . . and of natural ruler and subject, that both may be preserved. For that which can foresee by the exercise of mind is by nature intended to be lord and master, and that which can with its body give effect to such foresight is a subject, and by nature a slave. . . .

From the hour of their birth, some are marked out for subjection, others for rule. . . . And it is clear that the rule of the soul over the body, and of the mind and the rational element over the passionate, is natural and expedient; whereas the equality of the two or the rule of the inferior is always hurtful. . . . Again, the male is by nature superior, and the female inferior; and the one rules, and the other is ruled; this principle, of necessity, extends to all mankind. . . . The lower sort are by nature slaves, and it is better for them as for all inferiors that they should be under the rule of a master.

—ARISTOTLE, *POLITICS* (4TH CENTURY B.C.)

■ *The philosopher Friedrich Nietzsche, in his immortal* **Thus Spake Zarathustra,** *summarizes the Law of Female Obedience:*

As this day I went my way alone at the hour of sunset I met a little old woman who spake thus to my soul: "Much has Zarathustra spoken even to us women, but never has he spoken to us of woman."

And I answered her: "Of woman must one speak only to men."

"Speak also to me of woman," she said, "for I am old enough to forget it immediately."

And I, assenting, spake thus to the little old woman:

All in woman is a riddle, and all in woman has but one answer: that is child-bearing.

Man is for woman a means: the end is always the child. But what is woman for man?

There are two things a true man desires: danger and play. Therefore desires he woman as the most dangerous of playthings.

Man shall be trained for war, and woman for the recreation of the warrior: all else is folly. . . .

Let woman be a plaything pure and delicate as a jewel, illumined with the virtues of a world that is yet to come.

Let star-beams shine in your love! Let your hope be, Would I might give birth to the Superman! . . .

In your love let your honor be! Little else knows woman of honor. But let it be your honor ever to love more than you are loved, and never to be second. . . .

Man's happiness is, I will. Woman's happiness is, He will. . . .

Woman must obey to find depth to her surface. Surface is woman's nature, foam tossed to and fro on shallow water.

But deep is man's nature; his current flows in subterranean caverns: woman senses his power, but understands it not.

Then the little old woman answered me: "Many fine things says Zarathustra, especially for them that are young enough. A strange thing is this—Zarathustra knows little of women, yet is he right regarding them! Is this because with women nothing is impossible?

"And now take as thanks a little truth. I am old enough to speak it! Wrap it well and keep its mouth shut, or else it will cry over-loud, this little truth."

"Give me, woman, thy little truth," I said. And thus spake the little old woman:

"Thou goest to woman? Remember thy whip!"

Thus spake Zarathustra.

—FRIEDRICH NIETZSCHE, *THUS SPAKE ZARATHUSTRA* (1883)

Beat Your Wife

Brute force is Man's most potent weapon: he would be a fool not to use it.

Indeed, countless masculists today still employ this reliable method of persuasion.

A woman, an ass, and a walnut tree,
Bring the more fruit, the more beaten they be.
                              —ENGLISH PROVERB (16TH CENTURY)

Women should be struck regularly, like gongs.
                              —VICTOR IN NOEL COWARD, *PRIVATE LIVES* (1930)

A gentleman is someone who raises his hat before he beats his wife.
                              —BRITISH JOKE (ca. 1920)

Love well, whip well.
                              —BENJAMIN FRANKLIN, *POOR RICHARD* (1733)

I adore women. I am their total slave up to a certain point. I pamper them, cater to them, but when necessary, you have to bop 'em.
                              —TELLY SAVALAS, AMERICAN ACTOR (1975)

Good women are obedient, guarding in secret that which Allah has guarded. As for those from whom ye fear rebellion, admonish them and banish them to beds apart, and scourge them.

—MOHAMMAD, KORAN 4:34 (A.D. 626)

The way to handle wives, like the fellow says, is to catch 'em early, treat 'em rough, and tell 'em nothing!

—NAT HICKS IN SINCLAIR LEWIS, *MAIN STREET* (1920)

A woman is like a horse: he who can drive her is her master.

—KANURI PROVERB (NORTHERN NIGERIA AND THE SUDAN); SIMILARLY: ARGENTINE, BULGARIAN, ENGLISH, GENOESE, AND SPANISH PROVERBS

American girls are like horses, very independent. They have never been controlled by anybody. But if you can break them in, they are very grateful, as all women are.

—MICHAEL CAINE, BRITISH ACTOR (1974)

A bone for my dog; a stick for my wife.

—GALICIAN PROVERB

■ *The privilege of receiving manly discipline is not restricted to bad women.*

As both a good horse and a bad horse heed the spur,
so both a good woman and a bad woman need the stick.

—ITALIAN PROVERB

Beat your wife on the wedding day, and your married life will be happy.

—JAPANESE PROVERB

A bride received into the home is like a horse that you have just bought: you break her in by constantly mounting her and by continually beating her.

—CHINESE PROVERB

■ *The centerpiece of the traditional Russian wedding ceremony consists of the bride's father symbolically tapping the bride three times with a prettily decorated miniature whip, which he presents to the bridegroom, who then taps the bride in turn. The bride demonstrates her appreciation by kissing the shoe of her new master. This charming ritual is reflected in much folk wisdom:*

The more you beat your wife, the better will be the soup.
Beat a woman with a hammer and you'll make gold.
Beat your wife with the butt of an axe; if she falls down, sniffs and gasps, she is deceiving: give her some more.
A wife is not a pot, she will not break so easily.
A wife may love a husband who never beats her, but she does not respect him.

—RUSSIAN PROVERBS

■ *Traditional insight ascribes many benefits, both physical and spiritual, to the invigorating exercise of wife-beating.*

He who knocks his wife about properly will be forgiven a hundred sins.

—ESTONIAN PROVERB

He that drinks will get fat; he that loves will be healthy; and he that beats his wife will be saved.

A wife is like mint; the more you chop it, the sweeter it smells.

He who loves much beats hard.

—POLISH PROVERBS

■ *"Real men" do not fear to acknowledge the sexual component of woman-bashing:*

I felt a mean rage in my feet. It was as if in killing her, the act had been too gentle. . . . I had an impulse to go up to her and kick her ribs, grind my heel on her nose, drive the point of my shoe into her temple and kill her again, kill her good this time, kill her right. I stood there shuddering from the power of this desire.

—CROFT (NARRATOR) IN NORMAN MAILER, *AN AMERICAN DREAM* (1965)

■ *However, sophisticated patriarchs do not administer discipline indiscriminately.*

When you see your wife commit an offense, do not rush at her with insults and violent blows: rather, first correct the wrong lovingly and pleasantly, and sweetly teach her not to do it again so as not to offend God, injure her soul, or bring shame upon herself and you. . . .

But if your wife is of a servile disposition and has a crude and shifty spirit, so that pleasant words have no effect, scold her sharply, bully and terrify her. And if this still doesn't work . . . take up a stick and beat her soundly, for it is better to punish the body and correct the soul than to damage the soul and spare the body. But notice, I say, that you shouldn't beat her just because she does not get things ready exactly as you would like them, or for some other unimportant reason or minor failing. You should beat her, I say, only when she commits a serious wrong: for example, if she blasphemes against God or a saint, if she mutters the devil's name, if she likes being at the window and lends a ready ear to dishonest young men, or if she has taken to bad habits or bad company, or commits some other wrong that is a mortal sin. Then readily beat her, not in rage but out of charity and concern for her soul, so that the beating will redound to your merit and her good.

—FRIAR CHERUBINO DA SIENA, *RULES OF MARRIAGE* (1489)

Disobedient wives should be severely whipped, though not in anger. . . . A good wife should [likewise] be taught by her husband, by using the whip to her from time to time, but nicely, in secret, and in a polite fashion, avoiding blows of the fist which cause bruises.

—MONK SYLVESTER, *DOMOSTROI (HOUSEHOLD MANAGEMENT CODE;* RUSSIAN, 1556)

It is a well-known fact that you can strike your wife's bottom if you wish, but you must not strike her face. . . . Reasonable chastisement should be the duty of every husband if his wife disobeys.

—GEORGE MACKAY, SHERIFF OF KINGHORN, SCOTLAND (1975)

■ *The bulk of patriarchal law sustains this moderate view of female chastisement.*

The husband hath by law power and dominion over his wife, and may keep her by force, within the bounds of duty, and may beat her, but not in a violent or cruel manner.

—SIR FRANCIS BACON, *MAXIMS OF THE LAW* (1630)

A man may castigate his wife and beat her for her correction, for the lord must punish his own, as is written in Gratian's *Decretum*.

—ANON., *THEOLOGICAL DICTIONARY* (ca. 1300)

He may chastise her temperately, for she is of his household . . . unless he be a clergyman, in which case he may chastise her more severely.

—GRATIAN, *DECRETUM* (1140)

You may beat your wife as much as you like providing the stick is no bigger than your thumb.

—CHINESE LEGAL PROVERB

Every husband may beat his wife when she disobeys his commands, or when she curses him, or contradicts him—provided he do it moderately, and not to the extent of causing her death.

—PHILIPPE DE BEAUMANOIR, *CUSTOMS OF THE PEOPLE OF BEAUVAIS* (ca. 1285)

■ *Of course, it is completely within the female's power to spare herself the indignity of corporal punishment.*

Here is an example to every good woman that she suffer and endure patiently, nor strive with her husband, nor give him any displeasance, nor answer him before strangers, as did once a woman who did answer her husband before strangers with short words; and he smote her with his fist down to the earth; and then with his foot he struck her in her visage and brake her nose, and all her life after she had her nose crooked, the which so spoiled and disfigured her visage after, that she might not for shame show her face, it was so foul blemished. And this she had for her evil language that she was wont to say to her husband. And therefore the wife ought to suffer, and let the husband have the words, and to be master, for that is her duty.

—GEOFFREY DE LA TOUR DE LANDRY, *BOOK OF THE KNIGHT OF THE TOWER* (1371)

If a woman speaks . . . disrespectfully to a man, that woman's mouth is crushed with a fired brick.

—EDICT OF URUKAGINA, KING OF SUMER (ca. 2350 B.C.)

■ *In more enlightened societies, the woman may even be eligible for rehabilitation.*

Married women . . . may be entered or detained in the [mental] hospital at the request of the husband or guardian . . . without the evidence of insanity required in other cases.

—ILLINOIS LAW (1851)

■ *But not even the most indulgent husband may forgive a capital offense. Female crimes punishable by death are delineated in the statutes of all civilized societies.*

The "First Law of Marriage," promulgated by Romulus when he founded Rome in 753 B.C.:

. . . obliged married women, as having no other refuge, to conform themselves entirely to the temper of their husbands, and husbands to rule their wives as necessary and inseparable possessions. . . .

But if she did any wrong, the injured party was her judge, and determined the degree of her punishment. Other offenses, however, were judged by her relatives together with her husband; among them was adultery, or where it was found she had drunk wine . . . for Romulus permitted them to punish both these acts with death, as being the gravest offenses women could be guilty of. . . . And both these offenses continued for a long time to be punished by the Romans with merciless severity. The wisdom of this law concerning wives is attested by the length of time it was in force; for it is agreed that during the space of five hundred and twenty years no marriage was ever dissolved at Rome.

—DIONYSIUS OF HALICARNASSUS, *THE ROMAN ANTIQUITIES* (ca. 25 B.C.)

Egnatius Metellus . . . beat his wife to death because she had drunk some wine; and this murder, far from leading to his being censured, was not even blamed. People considered her punishment as proper expiation for her offense against the laws of sobriety: for any woman who drinks wine immoderately closes her heart to every virtue and opens it to every vice.

—VALERIUS MAXIMUS, *FACTA ET DICTA MEMORABILIA* (ca. A.D. 10)

■ *Female adultery, a violation of male property rights, is the ultimate offense against patriarchal civilization. Limitations of space restrict us to a mere sampling of laws regulating this heinous crime.*

A woman who commits adultery with a man of a lower caste, the king shall cause to be devoured by dogs in a public place.

—GAUTAMA, *THE SACRED LAWS* (HINDU SCRIPTURE, ca. A.D. 350)

If you should take your wife in adultery, you may with impunity put her to death without a trial; but if you should commit adultery or indecency, she must not presume to lay a finger on you, nor does the law allow it.

—MARCUS CATO, *ON THE DOWRY* (ca. 200 B.C.)

If a woman and her adulterer are killed by her husband or fiancé, he shall pay no fine for the homicide, nor be sentenced to death.

—SPANISH LAW (1240)

A man may with impunity kill his wife, mother, daughter, sister, aunt, niece, or cousin on his father's side if he believes her to be guilty of adultery.

—IRAQI LAW (PASSED BY IRAQ'S REVOLUTIONARY COMMAND COUNCIL, 1990)

■ *More progressive societies have prescribed milder penalties than death for the crime of female adultery. A legal ruling by Byzantine Emperor Leo the Wise:*

Of all sacrilegious abominations, the crime of adultery, in Our opinion, deserves a punishment no less severe than that for murder. . . . However, since We favor the humanitarian approach, We confirm the sentence set forth by later legislators, that both guilty parties should have their noses slit. Therefore let that remain the penalty for this crime.

But since the husband may not go uncompensated, he may retain his wife's dowry as consolation. . . . Furthermore, the wife must not be permitted to make a mockery of marriage and receive, along with the slitting of her nose, the right to consort freely with libertines; rather let her be shut up in a convent in lifetime expiation of her crime.

—LEO THE WISE, *NOVELS OF LEO* (ca. A.D. 900)

■ *An Italian city ordinance:*

If [the city's magistrates] find that a woman is having adulterous relations with a married man, be their liaison open or secret, they must have her severely flogged through the city streets and suburbs and then exile her for three years. As evidence against women of this sort, let public opinion and their reputation suffice.

—*STATUTES OF PERUGIA* (1342)

■ *Solon (sixth century B.C.):*

Solon, the famous lawgiver, has written in ancient and solemn manner concerning orderly conduct on the part of women. For the woman who is taken in the act of adultery he does not allow to adorn herself, nor even to attend the public sacrifices lest by mingling with innocent women she corrupt them. But if she does attend, or does adorn herself, he commands that any man who meets her shall tear off her garments, strip her of her ornaments, and beat her (only he may not kill or maim her); for the lawgiver seeks to disgrace such a woman and make her life not worth living.

—AESCHINES, "AGAINST TIMARCHUS" (365 B.C.)

■ *It follows that a man who fails to enforce such laws is himself a guilty party.*

Those are guilty of the crime of pimping who allow their wives taken in adultery to remain in marriage.

—ROMAN LAW (A.D. 200) INCORPORATED INTO THE *CODE OF JUSTINIAN* (ca. A.D. 550)

The husband who is cognizant of, and condones, his wife's adultery shall be flogged and exiled.

—BYZANTINE LAW, *ECLOGA PRIVATA AUCTA* (A.D. 726)

■ *A more liberal view allows the adulterous man to share the blame with the guilty woman.*

If a man has taken a man with his wife, and charge and proof have been brought against him, both of them shall be put to death; there is no liability therefor. . . . If the woman's husband puts his wife to death, then he shall put the man to death; if he has cut off his wife's nose, he shall make the man a eunuch and the whole of his face shall be mutilated.

—MIDDLE ASSYRIAN LAW (15TH TO 11TH CENTURIES B.C.)

If a father, either at his own house or at that of his son-in-law who has applied to him in the matter, has caught anyone committing adultery with his daughter, she being at the time in his power or having passed, with his sanction, out of his power into that of her husband, he is permitted to slay the adulterer without risk of prosecution, provided that he slays the daughter immediately. . . .

But if he does not kill the daughter but only the adulterer, he is guilty of murder.

—ROMAN LAW, *LEX JULIA DE ADULTERIIS* (18 B.C.)

Homicide is justifiable when committed by the husband upon one taken in the act of adultery with the wife, provided the killing takes place before the parties to the act have separated.

—TEXAS LAW (1961)

■ *The woman's collusion or noncollusion in the crime is not the issue.*

When a woman has been enjoyed against her will, she shall be kept in the house well guarded, smeared [with ashes], lying on a low couch, and receiving bare maintenance only.

To atone for her sin, she shall be caused to perform the Krikkhra or Parâka penance, in case she had intercourse with her equal in caste; but if she has been enjoyed by a man of inferior caste, she shall be abandoned and put to death.

When a woman comes to a man's house and excites his concupiscence by touching him or the like acts, she shall be punished. . . . Her nose, lips, and ears having been cut off, she shall be paraded in the streets and plunged into water; or she shall be torn to pieces by dogs in a public place frequented by many persons.

—BRIHASPATI, *THE SACRED LAWS* (HINDU SCRIPTURE, 1ST CENTURY A.D.)

Women Are Masochistic

Women enjoy *manly discipline. Therefore it is a kindness, not a cruelty, to put it to them.*

By extolling masochism as the feminine ideal, poets, philosophers, and psychologists certify that a woman who is not masochistic is not a true woman. Once women are convinced they are masochists, it is no longer necessary to beat them: they "discipline" themselves.

At last a woman who admits it! . . . Something that women have always refused till now to admit . . . that they never cease obeying their nature, the call of their blood, that everything in them, even their minds, is sex. That they have constantly to be nourished, constantly washed and made up, constantly beaten. That all they need is a good master, one who is not too lax or kind. . . . In short, that we must, when we go to see them, take a whip along.

—JEAN PAULHAN, "HAPPINESS IN SLAVERY," PREFACE TO *THE STORY OF O* (1954)

What women want is not to be treated with respect and care. They want to be treated like shit. They seem to like it.

—JOHN STEED, BRITISH RAPIST/MURDERER (1986)

She should be humble, who would please;
And she must suffer, who can love.

—MATTHEW PRIOR, "CHLOE JEALOUS" (ca. 1715)

■ *O what makes women lovely?*

O what makes women lovely? Virtue, faith, and gentleness in suffering: an endurance through scorn or trial; these call beauty forth, give it the stamp celestial, and admit it into sisterhood with angels.

—SIR NATHANIEL BRENT (ca. 1640)

Her soul, that once with pleasure shook,
Did any eyes her beauty own,
Now wonders how they dare to look
On what belongs to him alone;
The indignity of taking gifts
Exhilarates her loving breast;
A rapture of submission lifts
Her life into celestial rest;
There's nothing left of what she was;
Back to the babe the woman dies,
And all the wisdom that she has
Is to love him for being wise.

—COVENTRY PATMORE, *THE ANGEL IN THE HOUSE* (1856)

For men must work, and women must weep,
And the sooner it's over, the sooner to sleep.

—CHARLES KINGSLEY, "THE THREE FISHERS" (1856)

■ *These delightful sentiments do not obviate the need for rigorous analysis.*

There is one particularly constant relation between femininity and instinctual life which we do not want to overlook. The suppression of women's aggressiveness which is prescribed for them constitutionally and imposed on them socially favors the development of powerful masochistic impulses, which succeed, as we know, in binding erotically the destructive trends which have been diverted inwards. Thus masochism, as people say, is truly feminine. But if, as happens so often, you meet with masochism in men, what is left to you but to say that these men exhibit very plain feminine traits?

—SIGMUND FREUD, "FEMININITY" (1933)

[In cases of "nervous disease"] the infantile psychic picture often shows striking intensification of traits otherwise normal, such as infantile helplessness, the need for cuddling, for tenderness; and these then develop into anxiety, fear of being alone, timidity, shyness, fear of strangers and unknown people, hypersensitiveness to pain, prudishness, permanent fear of punishment and fear of the consequences of every act—in short into characteristics that impart *unmistakable feminine traits* to the boy. . . .

The normal craving of the child for nestling, the exaggerated submissiveness of the neurotically disposed individual, the feeling of weakness, of inferiority protected by hyper-sensitiveness, the realization of actual futility, the sense of being permanently pushed aside and of being at a disadvantage, all these are gathered together into a feeling of femininity. On the contrary, active strivings . . . the pursuit of self-

gratification, the stirring up of instincts and passions are thrown challengingly forward as a masculine protest. . . .

The meaning of this desire for power is: *I want to be a man.* It permeates both boys and girls to such a frightful degree that we are *from the very first, forced to assume that this attitude came to the front to counterbalance the non-pleasurable sensation of not being masculine.* . . . Every form of activity and aggression, of power, riches, triumph, sadism, disobedience, crime are falsely evaluated as masculine just as in the grown-up's world of ideas. As feminine are reckoned suffering, waiting, enduring, weakness, and *all masochistic tendencies.*

—ALFRED ADLER, "PSYCHICAL HERMAPHRODISM AND THE MASCULINE PROTEST" (1912)

Young women often ask whether they can "have an identity" before they know whom they will marry and for whom they will make a home. Granted that something in the young woman's identity must keep itself open for the peculiarities of the man to be joined and of the children to be brought up, I think that much of a young woman's identity is already defined in her kind of attractiveness and in the selective nature of her search for the man (or men) by whom she wishes to be sought.

—ERIK H. ERIKSON, "WOMANKIND AND THE INNER SPACE" (1965)

■ *Men "create" women.*

A woman can be anything that the man who loves her would have her be.

—SANDYS IN SIR JAMES M. BARRIE, *TOMMY AND GRIZEL* (1900)

It is the male that gives charms to womankind, that produces an air in their faces, a grace in their motions, a softness in their voices, and a delicacy in their complexions.

—JOSEPH ADDISON, *THE SPECTATOR* (JULY 17, 1712)

Women have no moral sense; they rely for their behavior upon the men they love.

—JEAN DE LA BRUYÈRE, *CARACTÈRES DE THÉOPHRASTE* (1688)

■ *An eminent philosopher describes the political implications of woman's "Will to Subjection":*

If [a woman] is married, her whole dignity depends upon her being completely subjected, and seeming to be so subjected, to her husband. . . . She has the power to withdraw her freedom, if she could have the will to do so. But that is the very point; she cannot rationally will to be free. Her relation to her husband being publicly known, she must, moreover, will to appear to all whom she knows as utterly subjected to, and utterly lost in, the man of her choice.

Hence her husband is the administrator of all her rights and she wishes those rights asserted only in so far as he wishes it. . . .

Women are ineligible for public office for the following simple reasons. Public officials are responsible to the state; hence they must be perfectly free and dependent always only upon their own free will. . . . Hence the exclusive condition under which a woman might become eligible for public office would be in a promise not to marry. But no rational woman can give such a promise, nor can the state rationally

accept it. For woman is destined to love. . . . But when she loves, it is her duty to marry and the state must not create obstacles to this. Now if a woman holding public office were to marry, two possibilities would follow. First, she might not subject herself to her husband in matters regarding her official duties, which would be utterly against female dignity, for she cannot say then that she has given herself up wholly to her husband. . . . Or, secondly, she might subject herself utterly to her husband, as nature and morality require. But in that case she would cease to be the official and he would become it. The office would become his by marriage, like the rest of the wife's property and rights. But this the state cannot allow.

—JOHANN GOTTLIEB FICHTE, *THE SCIENCE OF RIGHTS*
(ca. 1800)

■ *We can begin to understand the custom of a bride's father giving her away in marriage:*

[It] putteth women in mind of a duty whereunto the very imbecility of their nature and sex doth bind them, namely to be always directed, guided and ordered by others.

—RICHARD HOOKER, *OF THE LAWS OF ECCLESIASTICAL POLITIE* (1597)

■ *Because, as a matter of course:*

Water and women go as men direct them.
—BULGARIAN AND MONTENEGRIN PROVERBS

Men have marble, women waxen, minds.
—WILLIAM SHAKESPEARE, *THE RAPE OF LUCRECE* (1594)

What cannot a neat knave with a smooth tale make a woman believe?
—FERDINAND OF CALABRIA IN JOHN WEBSTER, *THE DUCHESS OF MALFI* (ca. 1613)

O silly woman, full of innocence,
Full of pity, of truth, and of conscience,
What maketh you to men to trusten so?
—GEOFFREY CHAUCER, *LEGEND OF GOOD WOMEN*, "DIDO" (1385–86)

■ *Now there's a question that's easy to answer.*

Woman is essentially a Phallus worshipper . . . permeated with a fear like that of a bird for a snake. . . . It has never until now been made clear where the bondage of women lies; it is in the sovereign, all too welcome power wielded on them by the Phallus.
—OTTO WEININGER, *SEX AND CHARACTER* (1903)

■ *It's all so simple!*

The only way to resolve a situation with a girl is to jump on her, and things will work out.
—LEE MARVIN, AMERICAN ACTOR, INTERVIEW (1984)

Rules are like women. They are meant to be violated.
                    —DENYS DIONNE, QUEBEC COURT JUSTICE (1990)

A little bit of rape is good for man's soul.
                    —NORMAN MAILER, SPEECH AT BERKELEY, CALIFORNIA (1972)

The difference between rape and seduction is salesmanship.
—BILL CARPENTER, MAYOR OF INDEPENDENCE, MISSOURI (1990)

Every woman loves the idea of a sheikh carrying her off on his white horse and raping her in his tent. It's a basic feminine instinct.
—OMAR SHARIF, EGYPTIAN ACTOR, INTERVIEW (1981)

■ *Rape is the only violent crime whose victims are routinely advised to "relax and enjoy it."*

The weather is like rape: if it's inevitable, just relax and enjoy it.
—CLICHÉ REPEATED BY CLAYTON WILLIAMS, REPUBLICAN CANDIDATE FOR
GOVERNOR OF TEXAS (1990);
SIMILARLY: TEX ANTOINE, WABC-TV WEATHERMAN (1976)

■ *This is not a new joke.*

A wench accused a fellow for a rape. The judge asked her whether he offered her any violence, as to bind her hands, or otherwise.

"Yes," saith she, "he bound my hands, and he would have bound my legs too, but he could not bring them together. I thank God I kept them far enough asunder."
—BRITISH JOKE IN ANON., *A BANQUET OF JEASTS* (1630)

■ *Some amatory advice from the Casanova of the classical world:*

Who that is wise would not mingle kisses with coaxing words? Though she give them not, yet take the kisses she does not give. Perhaps she will struggle at first, and cry "You villain!" yet she will wish to be beaten in the struggle. . . . He who has taken kisses, if he

take not the rest beside, will deserve to lose even what was granted.
. . . You may use force; women like you to use it; they often wish to
give unwillingly what they like to give. She whom a sudden assault
has taken by storm is pleased, and counts the audacity as a compliment.
But she who, when she might have been compelled, departs un-
touched, though her looks feign joy, will yet be sad.

—OVID, *THE ART OF LOVE* (ca. A.D. 5)

■ *Some more modern descriptions of this phenomenon:*

Most women . . . enjoy the display of manly force even when it turns
against themselves.

—EDWARD WESTERMARCK, *THE FUTURE OF MARRIAGE IN WESTERN CIVILISATION* (1936)

Women delight in experiencing physical pain when inflicted by a lover.

—HAVELOCK ELLIS, *STUDIES IN THE PSYCHOLOGY OF SEX* (1901)

Women love to be sat on and conquered. They love to be bossed.

—MAXIMILIAN SCHELL, AUSTRIAN ACTOR (1978)

Women are called womanly only when they regard themselves as existing solely for the use of men.

—GEORGE BERNARD SHAW, PREFACE TO *GETTING MARRIED* (1908)

■ *A psychoanalyst and a sociologist explain why feminism failed
(1947):*

Feminism, despite the external validity of its political program and
most (not all) of its social program, was at its core a deep illness. . . .
The dominant direction of feminine training and development today

. . . discourages just those traits necessary to the attainment of sexual pleasure: receptivity and passiveness, a willingness to accept dependence without fear or resentment, with a deep inwardness and readiness for the final goal of sexual life—impregnation. . . .

It is not in the capacity of the female organism to attain feelings of well-being by the route of male achievement. . . . It was the error of the feminists that they attempted to put women on the essentially male road of exploit, off the female road of nurture. . . .

The psychosocial rule that begins to take form, then, is this: the more educated the woman is, the greater chance there is of sexual disorder, more or less severe. The greater the disordered sexuality in a given group of women, the fewer children do they have. . . . Fate has granted them the boon importuned by Lady Macbeth; they have been unsexed, not only in the matter of giving birth, but in their feelings of pleasure.

—M. FARNHAM AND F. LUNDBERG, *MODERN WOMAN: THE LOST SEX* (1947)

■ *These principles authenticate the natural harmony between the female's passive sexual nature and her feeble abilities.*

A woman is a valley, a man is a peak;
a man enters the woman, the woman simply allows;
a man is an aggression, a woman is a receptivity;
a man tries to do, a woman simply waits for things to happen. . . .
Look at a woman. She is balanced. Her needs are small:
somebody to love, somebody to be loved by, food, shelter,
a little warmth around, a home—finished.
And she is not worried about anything:
no woman has created any science;
no woman has founded any religion.

—BHAGWAN SHREE RAJNEESH, "COMMENTARY ON LAO TZU" (1976)

A home, a fireside, a husband, children, a little church-going, a little reading of innocuous writers, thirty years of small joys and small sorrows, thirty years of faithful love and careful housewifery, may mean a commonplace and undistinguished life. On the other hand, all the wisdom, and all the philosophy in the world, can suggest no better, or nobler, or more satisfying life for a woman.

—T. W. H. CROSLAND, *LOVELY WOMAN* (1903)

■ *And speaking of female pleasure:*

When a woman is merely a woman—when she winds herself round and round men's hearts with her smiles and sobs and services and caressing endearments—then she is happy. Of what use to her are learning and great achievements?

—CHITRA IN RABINDRANATH TAGORE, *CHITRA* (1913)

Dusting, darning, drudging, nothing is great or small,
Nothing is mean or irksome, love will hallow it all.

—WALTER CHALMERS SMITH, *HILDA AMONG THE BROKEN GODS* (1878)

It is annoying and impossible to suffer proud women, because in general Nature has given men proud and high spirits, while it has made women humble in character and submissive, more apt for delicate things than for ruling. Therefore, it should not be surprising if God's wrath is swifter and the sentence more severe against proud women whenever it happens that they surpass the boundaries of their weakness.

—GIOVANNI BOCCACCIO, "NIOBE" (ca. 1360)

■ *Six centuries later, Dr. Benjamin Spock agrees:*

Women are usually more patient in working at unexciting, repetitive tasks. . . . Women on the average have more passivity in the inborn core of their personality. . . . I believe women are designed in their deepest instincts to get more pleasure out of life—not only sexually but socially, occupationally, maternally—when they are not aggressive. To put it another way I think that when women are encouraged to be competitive too many of them become disagreeable.

—DR. BENJAMIN M. SPOCK, *DECENT AND INDECENT* (1969)

So I wonder a woman, the Mistress of Hearts,
Should ascend to aspire to be Master of Arts;
A Ministering Angel in Woman we see,
And an Angel need covet no other Degree.

—LORD NEAVES, "O WHY SHOULD A WOMAN NOT GET A DEGREE?" (ca. 1868)

The Virtuous Woman

Since woman's sin and shame, and her threat to Man's complacency, reside in her private parts, it follows that there is only one possible female virtue.

Women have one great advantage: it is sufficient for them to cultivate a single virtue if they wish to be well thought of. . . . If a woman keeps her body intact, all her other defects are hidden and she can hold her head high.

—PHILIPPE DE NAVARRE, *LES QUÂTRE ÂGES DE L'HOMME* (ca. 1260)

With regard to sexual relations, we should note that in giving herself to intercourse, the [unmarried] girl renounces her honour. . . . Girls have their essential destiny in marriage and there only.

—GEORG WILHELM FRIEDRICH HEGEL, *PHILOSOPHY OF RIGHT* (1821)

A virtuous woman, too, is like a mirror of clear shining crystal, liable to be tarnished and dimmed by every breath that touches it. She must be treated as relics are; adored, not touched. She must be protected and prized as one protects and prizes a fair garden full of roses and flowers, the owner of which allows no one to trespass or pluck a blossom; enough for others that from afar and through the iron grating they may enjoy its fragrance and its beauty.

—LOTHARIO IN MIGUEL DE CERVANTES, *DON QUIXOTE* (1605)

A woman takes off her claim to respect along with her garments.

—HERODOTUS, *HISTORY* (ca. 450 B.C.)

Authorities, both old and recent,
Direct that women must be decent.

—JONATHAN SWIFT, *STREPHON AND CHLOE* (1731)

■ *The consequences of female unchastity are permanent.*

The trav'ler, if he chance to stray,
May turn uncensur'd to his way;
Polluted streams again are pure,
And deepest wounds admit a cure;
But woman! no redemption knows,
The wounds of honour never close.

—EDWARD MOORE, *FABLES FOR THE LADIES* (1750)

A female by one trangression forfeits her place in society forever; if once she falls, it is the fall of Lucifer.

—REV. CHARLES CALEB COLTON, *LACON* (1820)

A woman who has lost her chastity will shrink from no other crime.

—TACITUS, *ANNALS* (ca. A.D. 100)

■ *What of women who violate the Law of Chastity?*

Women who have submitted to public prostitution . . . are so corrupt that they can have no protection from the law.

—MONTESQUIEU, *THE SPIRIT OF LAWS* (1748)

In dealing with this unhappy being [the prostitute], and with all of her sex who have violated the law of chastity, the public opinion of most Christian countries pronounces a sentence of extreme severity. In the Anglo-Saxon nations especially, a single fault of this kind is sufficient, at least in the upper and middle classes, to affix an indelible brand which no time, no virtue, no penitence can wholly efface.

—WILLIAM EDWARD HARTPOLE LECKY, *HISTORY OF EUROPEAN MORALS* (1869)

■ *It is clear that the virtues and sins of women differ completely from those of men.*

The virtues of a naturally higher class are more noble than those of a naturally lower class; thus the virtues of men are nobler than those of women.

—ARISTOTLE, *RHETORIC* (4TH CENTURY B.C.)

In man mortal sins are venial; in woman venial sins are mortal.

—ITALIAN PROVERB

A maid that laughs is half taken.

—ENGLISH PROVERB (17TH CENTURY)

When lovely woman stoops to folly,
    And finds too late that men betray,
What charm can soothe her melancholy,
    What art can wash her guilt away?
The only art her guilt to cover,
    To hide her shame from every eye,
And give repentance to her lover,
    And wring his bosom, is—to die.

—OLIVER GOLDSMITH, *THE VICAR OF WAKEFIELD* (1766)

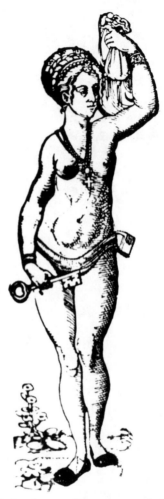

■ *The failure of virginity is a serious matter indeed.*

Starving to death is a small matter, but for a woman to lose her chastity is a great calamity.

—CONFUCIAN PROVERB (ca. A.D. 800)

If any man take a wife, and go in unto her, and hate her, and give occasions of speech against her, and say, "I took this woman, and when I came to her, I found her not a maid" . . . [and] if this thing be true, and the tokens of virginity be not found for the damsel: then they shall bring out the damsel to the door of her father's house, and the men of her city shall stone her with stones that she die.

—OLD TESTAMENT, DEUTERONOMY 22:13–21 (REVISED 7TH CENTURY B.C.)

■ *This is why daughters are so bothersome to keep about the house.*

Daughters and dead fish are no keeping wares.

—ENGLISH PROVERB (18TH CENTURY)

A house full of daughters is like a cellar full of sour beer.

—DUTCH PROVERB

Eighteen goddess-like daughters are not equal to one son with a hump.

—CHINESE PROVERB

A daughter is an embarrassing and ticklish possession.

—MENANDER, *PERINTHIS* (ca. 300 B.C.)

It is easier to watch over a sackful of fleas than one young girl.

—GERMAN, HUNGARIAN, AND POLISH PROVERBS

People ask me how many children I have and I say one boy and seven mistakes.

—MUHAMMAD ALI, WORLD HEAVYWEIGHT BOXING CHAMPION (1985)

■ *Virginity has been glorified to the point of deification.*

Now speaking to virgins: You are the flower of the church, the masterpiece of spiritual grace, the happy blossoming of nature . . . the
most brilliant portion of Christ's flock. . . . When He says that there
are many mansions in His Father's house, He means that some places
there are better than others. Those places are for you, virgins.

—ST. CYPRIAN, *DE HABITU VIRGINUM* (ca. A.D. 235)

Virginity stands as far above marriage as the heavens above the earth.

—ST. JOHN CHRYSOSTOM, *ON VIRGINITY; AGAINST HOLY MARRIAGE* (ca. A.D. 380)

I praise wedlock, I praise marriage, but only because they give me
virgins.

—ST. JEROME, *EPISTLE 22* (ca. A.D. 420)

Wives and mats are best when new.

—JAPANESE PROVERB

■ *Even married women must cultivate chastity.*

Fair daughters . . . throughout your married life you ought to fast
three days a week to keep your flesh down and yourselves chaste.

—GEOFFREY DE LA TOUR DE LANDRY, *BOOK OF THE KNIGHT OF THE TOWER* (1371)

When a woman, in her husband's absence, seeks to display her beauty,
mark her as a wanton.

—ELECTRA IN EURIPIDES, *ELECTRA* (413 B.C.)

Herodotus was mistaken when he said a woman takes off her modesty
along with her clothes. Quite the opposite, she puts on modesty in

their place, and the husband and wife show the greatest modesty as a token of their very great love for each other. . . .

The wife ought not to have any feelings of her own but join with her husband in his moods whether serious, playful, thoughtful, or joking.

Should a man in private life be without control or guidance in his pleasures and commit some indiscretion with a prostitute or servant girl, the wife should not take it hard or be angry, reasoning that because of his respect for her, he does not include her in his drunken parties, excesses, and wantonness with other women. . . .

Not gold, not gems, not scarlet, make a woman more proper, but whatever invests her appearance with dignity, discipline, and shame.

—PLUTARCH, "CONJUGAL PRECEPTS" (ca. A.D. 110)

■ *The virtuous wife has other duties as well.*
From the **Kāma Sūtra,** *"About a Wife":*

A virtuous woman who has affection for her husband should act in conformity with his wishes as if he were a divine being. . . . She should keep the whole house well cleaned, and arrange flowers in various parts of it, and make the floor smooth and polished so as to give the whole a neat and becoming appearance. . . .

A wife should always avoid the company of female beggars, female Buddhist mendicants, unchaste and roguish women, female fortune-tellers and witches. As regards meals, she should always consider what her husband likes and dislikes, and what things are good for him. . . . When she hears the sound of his footsteps coming home she should at once get up, and be ready to do whatever he may command her. . . .

In the event of any misconduct on the part of her husband, she should not blame him. . . . Lastly, she should avoid bad expressions, sulky looks, speaking aside, standing in the doorway and looking at passers-by. . . . And finally she should always keep her body, her teeth, her hair, and everything belonging to her tidy, sweet, and clean. . . .

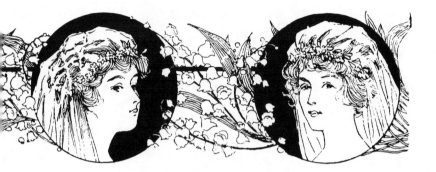

The wife . . . should lead a chaste life, devoted to her husband, and doing everything for his welfare. Women acting thus . . . generally keep their husbands devoted to them.

—VĀTSYĀYANA, *THE KĀMA SŪTRA OF VĀTSYĀYANA* (4TH CENTURY A.D.)

■ *More on how to hold a husband:*

Cherish your husband's person and make sure you keep him in clean linen, this being your office. For men have to look after things outside the home and husbands have to go abroad in all sorts of weather. . . . But he endures it all, taking consolation from thinking about the good care he will receive from his wife when he returns home, as she warms him by the fire, washes his feet, fetches him fresh shoes and stockings, good food and drink. . . .

Indeed, fair sister, these are the services that make a man wish for home and long to return to it. . . . And don't be quarrelsome but sweet, gentle and amiable. . . . And if you do all this, he will keep his heart for you and for the dear service you render him, and he will care nought for other houses or other women.

—ANON., *LE MENAGIER DE PARIS* (1393)

To be well dressed, in good humor, and cheerful in the command of her family, are the arts and sciences of female life.

—SIR RICHARD STEELE, *THE TATLER* (OCTOBER 1, 1709)

A young wife, in her own house, should be only a shadow and an echo.

—JAPANESE PROVERB

Marriage is very difficult. Very few of us are fortunate enough to marry multimillionaire girls with 39-inch busts who have undergone frontal lobotomies.

—TONY CURTIS, AMERICAN ACTOR (1980)

■ *Widows present a special problem. Having outlived their fathers and husbands, they present the specter of women living independent of male authority. This will never do.*

Honor widows that are widows indeed. . . . She that is a widow indeed, and desolate, trusteth in God, and continueth in supplications and prayers night and day. But she that liveth in pleasure is dead while she liveth.

—NEW TESTAMENT, 1 TIMOTHY 5:3–6 (ca. A.D. 50)

Widows, sir, are the most perverse creatures in the world.

—JOSEPH ADDISON, *THE SPECTATOR* (MARCH 25, 1712)

That wife is declared to be devoted to her husband who is afflicted when he is afflicted, pleased when he is happy, squalid and languid when he is absent, and who dies when he dies.

—BRIHASPATI, *THE SACRED LAWS* (HINDU SCRIPTURE, 1ST CENTURY A.D.)

A buxom widow must be either married, buried, or shut up in a convent.

—SPANISH PROVERB

An old woman and a new plough are nowhere better than in the earth.

—GERMAN PROVERB

■ *The perfectly ideal, impeccably virtuous woman (too rare, alas!) possesses neither sexuality nor personality, but only selfless devotion to pleasing Man.*

In an uncorrupted woman the sexual impulse does not manifest at all, but only love; and this love is the natural impulse of a woman to satisfy a man. . . .

The woman who thus surrenders her personality, and yet retains her full dignity in so doing, necessarily gives up to her lover all that she has. . . . Henceforth her life has become a part of the life of her lover. (This is aptly characterized by her assuming his name.) . . .

The state, by recognizing marriage . . . abandons all claims to consider woman as a legal person. The husband supplies her place; her marriage utterly annuls her.

—JOHANN GOTTLIEB FICHTE, *THE SCIENCE OF RIGHTS* (ca. 1800)

■ *From a selection of popular nineteenth-century sex manuals:*

It is a delusion under which many a previously incontinent man suffers, to suppose that in newly married life he will be required to treat his wife as he used to treat his mistresses. It is not so. . . . He need not fear that his wife will require the excitement, or in any respect imitate the ways of a courtesan. . . .

The majority of women (happily for them) are not very much troubled with sexual feelings of any kind. . . .

Many men, and particularly young men, form their ideas of women's feelings from what they notice early in life among loose or, at least, low and vulgar women. . . . Such women however give a very false idea of the condition of female sexual feelings in general. . . . The best mothers, wives, and managers of households, know little or nothing of sexual indulgences. Love of home, children, and domestic duties are the only passions they feel.

As a general rule, a modest woman seldom desires any sexual gratification for herself. She submits to her husband, but only to please him; and, but for the desire of maternity, would far rather be relieved from his attentions. No nervous or feeble young man need, therefore, be deterred from marriage by any exaggerated notion of the duties required from him. The married woman has no wish to be treated on the footing of a mistress.

—WILLIAM ACTON, M.D.,
THE FUNCTIONS AND DISORDERS OF THE REPRODUCTIVE ORGANS (1857)

A vulgar opinion prevails that [women] are creatures of like passions with ourselves; that they experience desires as ardent, and often as ungovernable. . . . Nothing is more utterly untrue. . . . Only in rare instances do women experience one-tenth of the sexual feeling which is familiar to most men.

—GEORGE H. NAPHEYS, M.D., *THE TRANSMISSION OF LIFE* (1878)

In men in general, the sexual desire is inherent and spontaneous and belongs to the condition of puberty. In the other sex the desire is dormant, or nonexistent till excited; always till excited by undue fa-

miliarities. . . . Women, whose position and education have protected them from exciting causes, constantly pass through life without being cognizant of the promptings of the senses.

—ANON., "PROSTITUTION" (1851)

■ *Others agree.*

In intercourse women feel much less pleasure than men do, but they feel it longer. If men feel a more intense pleasure, it is because their discharge is brusquer and provoked by a more acute excitement than that experienced by women.

—HIPPOCRATES (ca. 400 B.C.)

Woman is the lesser man, and all thy passions, match'd with mine
Are as moonlight unto sunlight, and as water unto wine.

—ALFRED, LORD TENNYSON, *LOCKSLEY HALL* (1842)

Her Proper Sphere

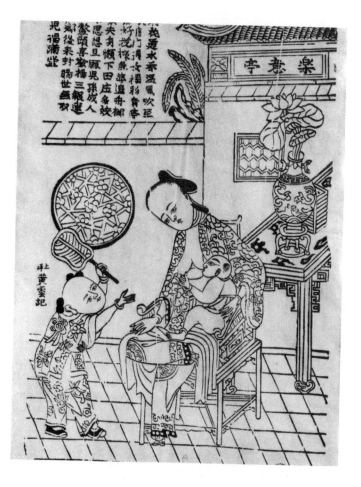

Considering the weaknesses of the female character—and the inconveniences men would suffer if the current social order were overturned—temptation can lead only to disgrace; and as the only sure guarantor of female virtue is a stiff padlock, all civilized peoples enforce the notion that "a woman's place is in the home."

A wife that expects to have a good name
Is always at home, as if she were lame.

—ENGLISH PROVERB (17TH CENTURY)

Have you ever learned the reason
   For the binding of your feet?
'Tis from fear that 'twill be easy
   To go out upon the street.

—CONFUCIAN CLASSIC FOR GIRLS (ca. A.D. 800)

Women and chickens get lost by wandering from house to house.

—HINDU PROVERB; SIMILARLY IN CERVANTES, DON QUIXOTE (1605)

Freedom spoils a good wife.

—RUSSIAN PROVERB

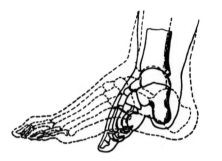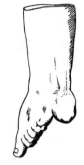

The home is the wife's world;
The world is the man's home.

—ESTONIAN PROVERB

A woman is to be from her house three times:
When she is christened, married, and buried.

—ENGLISH PROVERB (18TH CENTURY)

A woman is well only in the house or in the grave.

—AFGHANI PROVERB

■ *This is because women have no reason for existing other than to please men.*

She is not made to be the admiration of all, but the happiness of one.

—EDMUND BURKE (ca. 1750)

All a woman has to do in this world is contained within the duties of a daughter, a sister, a wife, and a mother.

—SIR RICHARD STEELE (ca. 1700)

[My wife] has a very major cause and a very major interest that is a very complex and consuming issue with her. And that's me.

—VICE PRESIDENT DAN QUAYLE (1989)

Phidias made the statue of Venus at Elis with one foot upon the shell of a tortoise, to signify the two great duties of a virtuous woman, which are to keep home and be silent.

—W. DE BRITAINE, *HUMAN PRUDENCE* (1726)

Women should be quiet. When people are talking, they ought to retire to the kitchen.

—W. H. AUDEN, *TABLE TALK* (1947)

A woman's place is in the wrong.

—JAMES THURBER (ca. 1940)

A woman's place is in the stove.

—MORT SAHL (ca. 1960)

A woman's place is in the bedroom.

—FERDINAND E. MARCOS, EX-PRESIDENT OF THE PHILIPPINES (1986)

■ *The dangers inherent in the female's appearance in public should not be underestimated.*

The female is an empty thing and easily swayed; she runs great risks when she is away from her husband. Therefore, keep your women in the house, keep them as close to yourself as you can, and come home often to oversee your affairs and to keep them in fear and trembling. Be sure they always have work to do in the house and never allow them to be idle.

—PAOLO DA CERTALDO, *HANDBOOK OF GOOD CUSTOMS* (ca. 1360)

No one can evade the fact, that in taking up a masculine calling, studying and working in a man's way, woman is doing something not wholly in agreement with, if not directly injurious to, her feminine nature. . . .

Female psychology is founded on the principle of Eros, the great binder and deliverer; while age-old wisdom ascribed Logos to man as his ruling principle.

—CARL JUNG, *CONTRIBUTIONS TO ANALYTICAL PSYCHOLOGY* (1928)

■ *Home life is healthy and cleansing for women.*

Pleasure is to women, what the sun is to the flower: if moderately enjoyed, it beautifies, it refreshes, and it improves; if immoderately, it withers, deteriorates, and destroys. But the duties of domestic life, exercised as they must be in retirement, and calling forth all the sensibilities of the female, are perhaps as necessary to the full development of her charms, as the shades and showers are to the rose, confirming its beauty, and increasing its fragrance.

—REV. CHARLES CALEB COLTON, *LACON* (1820)

O ye wives . . . stay in your houses. . . . Allah's wish is but to remove uncleanness from you, O Folk of the Household, and cleanse you with a thorough cleansing.

—MOHAMMAD, *KORAN* 33:32–33 (A.D. 628)

■ *There are questions of occupational suitability.*

Men have broad shoulders and narrow hips, and accordingly they possess intelligence. Women have narrow shoulders and broad hips. Women ought to stay at home; the way they were created indicates this, for they have broad hips and a wide fundament to sit upon (keep house and bear and raise children).

—MARTIN LUTHER, *TABLE TALK* (1531)

It is absurd to argue from an analogy with wild animals and say that men and women ought to engage in the same occupations, for animals do not do housework.

—ARISTOTLE, *POLITICS* (4TH CENTURY B.C.)

When a woman says she wants to go out and get a job to express herself it usually means she's hopelessly behind in the ironing.

—OLIVER REED, BRITISH ACTOR (1978)

Biologically and temperamentally, I believe, women were made to be concerned first and foremost with child care, husband care, and home care.

—DR. BENJAMIN M. SPOCK, IN *REDBOOK* (MARCH 1969)

The message of woman's emancipation is a message discovered solely by the Jewish intellect and its content is stamped with the same spirit. . . . Only when man himself is unsure in the perception of his task did the eternal instinct of self- and folk-preservation begin to revolt in women. . . . For her world is her husband, her family, her children and her home. . . .

Reason is dominant in man. He searches, analyzes, and often opens new immeasurable realms. But all things that are approached merely by reason are subject to change. Feeling in contrast is much more subtle than reason and woman is the feeling and therefore the stable element. . . .

I am convinced that the [National Socialist] Movement is understood better by none than the German woman. When our opponents imply that we in Germany have instituted a tyrannical regimentation of women, I can only confess that without the endurance and really loving devotion of woman to the Movement, I could never have led the Party to victory.

—ADOLF HITLER, SPEECH AT NUREMBERG (SEPTEMBER 8, 1934)

■ *Some commentators approvingly compare housewifery to slavery:*

The real housewife is at once a slave and a lady.

—BOSNIAN PROVERB

Nature intended women to be our slaves. . . . They are our property, we are not theirs. . . . They belong to us, just as a tree which bears fruit belongs to the gardener. What a mad idea to demand equality for women! . . . Women are nothing but machines for producing children.

—NAPOLEON BONAPARTE (1817)

A wife will be doubly attached if her chain is pleasant.

—EGYPTIAN PROVERB, CITED BY PTAH HOTEP (ca. 3000 B.C.)

Being married is the best prison for a woman. It is a marvelous jail.

—PIERRE CARDIN, FRENCH FASHION DESIGNER (1979)

■ *But others disagree.*

Woman . . . is not a slave, for she and her children are supported by her husband's work. She is not oppressed, for nature has ordained that she should live under the protection of the man while she fulfils her mission in life as mother. Woman is not man's intellectual equal; the man, on the other hand, cannot bear children. She is not an essential factor in the great work of civilisation; this is man's domain, for he is better fitted to grapple with spiritual problems than she is. . . .

Woman, man's necessary complement, the spiritual creation of man, has no right to the privileges of her husband, for she can only be called "the other half of humanity" by virtue of her numbers, proportionally she is merely the sixth part of a sixth. She should not, therefore, invade the labour market as long as it falls to the lot of the man to provide for his wife and family. And the fact should not be lost sight of that every time a woman wrests an appointment from a man, there is one more old maid or prostitute. . . .

The monomania of weak and inferior brains, that desire to equalise what can never be equal, was the cause of much mischief in my family.

—AUGUST STRINDBERG, *THE CONFESSION OF A FOOL* (AUTOBIOGRAPHICAL NOVEL, 1888)

■ *Later in this chapter we will again encounter the argument that when women work outside the home they deprive men of jobs and themselves of husbands, thereby causing poverty and prostitution, and weakening the body politic.*

Sigmund Freud's difficulties in establishing himself financially caused his marriage to Martha Bernays to be postponed for more than ten years. On several occasions Ms. Bernays offered to go to work, to enable them to end their lives of celibacy. The good doctor would not hear of it:

It is really a stillborn thought to send women into the struggle for existence exactly as men. If, for instance, I imagined my sweet gentle girl as a competitor it would only end in my telling her . . . that I am fond of her and that I implore her to withdraw from the strife into the calm incompetitive activity of my home. It is possible that changes in upbringing may suppress all a woman's tender attributes . . . and that she can then earn a livelihood like men. It is also possible that in such an event one would not be justified in mourning the passing away of the most delightful thing the world can offer us—our ideal of womanhood. I believe that all reforming action in law and education would break down in front of the fact that, long before the age at which a man can earn a position in society, Nature has determined a woman's destiny through beauty, charm and sweetness. Law and custom may have much more to give women that has been withheld from them, but the position of women will surely be what it is: in youth an adored darling and in mature years a loved wife.

—SIGMUND FREUD, LETTER TO HIS FIANCÉE (NOVEMBER 5, 1883)

■ *The needs and preferences of men are the natural determinants of social policy.*

Men do not like, and would not seek, to mate with an independent factor, who at any time could quit—or who at all times would be tempted to neglect—the tedious duties of training and bringing up children, and keeping the tradesmen's bills, and mending the linen, for the more lucrative returns of the desk or counter. It is not the interest of States, and it is not therefore true social policy, to encourage the existence . . . of women who are other than entirely dependent on man as well for subsistence as for protection and love.

—EDITORIAL, *THE SATURDAY REVIEW* (1859)

■ *The admission of women into religious life—where they run the risk of not being under the direct supervision of individual men—has always been controversial.*

From the founder of the Jesuit Order:

The spiritual direction of just three women is a task more arduous than the administration of an entire Order.

—ST. IGNATIUS LOYOLA, *SPIRITUAL EXERCISES* (1548)

■ *The Buddha himself, addressing his favorite disciple, predicted that the religion he founded would come to a premature end if women were allowed to practice it.*

Just, Ananda, as houses in which there are many women and but few men are easily violated by robber burglars; just so, Ananda, under whatever doctrine and discipline women are allowed to go out from the household life into the homeless state, that religion will not last long. And just, Ananda, as when the disease called mildew falls upon a field of rice in fine condition, that field of rice does not continue long; just so, Ananda, under whatsoever doctrine and discipline women are allowed to go forth from the household life into the homeless state, that religion will not last long.

—TRIPITAKA, *VINAYA-PITAKA* (BUDDHIST SCRIPTURE, ca. 80 B.C.)

■ *Any admission of women into public life is troubling.*

The grant of suffrage to women is repugnant to instincts that strike their roots deep in the order of nature. It runs counter to human reason, it flouts the teachings of experience and the admonitions of common sense.

—EDITORIAL, *THE NEW YORK TIMES* (FEBRUARY 7, 1915)

The only position for women in the Revolution is prone.

—STOKELY CARMICHAEL, AMERICAN POLITICAL REVOLUTIONARY (1969)

It is a grave error in your law that the position of women has been left unregulated. . . . No, the very half of the race which is generally predisposed by its weakness to undue secrecy and craft—the female sex— has been left to its disorders by the mistaken concession of the legislator. . . . Woman—left without chastening restraint—is not, as you might fancy, merely half the problem; nay, she is a twofold more than a twofold problem, in proportion as her native disposition is inferior to man's.

—PLATO, *LAWS* (ca. 345 B.C.)

■ *On admitting women into the armed forces:*

Women are hard enough to handle now, without giving them a gun.

—SENATOR BARRY GOLDWATER (1980)

■ *From a United States Supreme Court opinion holding that a woman can constitutionally be denied a license to practice law on the grounds of her sex:*

Man is, or should be, woman's protector and defender. The natural and proper timidity and delicacy which belongs to the female sex evidently unfits it for many of the occupations of civil life. The constitution of the family organization, which is founded in the divine ordinance, as well as in the nature of things, indicates the domestic sphere as that which properly belongs to the domain and functions of womanhood. The harmony, not to say identity, of interests and views, which belong, or should belong, to the family institution is repugnant to the idea of a woman adopting a distinct and independent career from that of her husband. . . .

The paramount destiny and mission of woman are to fulfill the noble and benign offices of wife and mother. This is the law of the Creator. And the rules of civil society must be adapted to the general constitution of things, and cannot be based upon exceptional cases.

—JUSTICE JOSEPH P. BRADLEY, *BRADWELL V. THE STATE* (1872)

■ *Another U.S. Supreme Court ruling:*

The Constitution does not require things which are different in fact or opinion to be treated in law as though they were the same.
—JUSTICE FELIX FRANKFURTER, *TIGNER V. TEXAS* (1940)

■ *The problem is that granting women political and economic rights creates the possibility of their assuming power. This will never do.*

No good ever came out of female domination. God created Adam master and lord of all living creatures, but Eve spoiled all.
—MARTIN LUTHER, *TABLE TALK* (1532)

Man to Gods image; *Eve,* to mans was made,
  Nor finde wee that God breath'd a soule in her.
Canons will not Church functions you invade,
  Nor lawes to civill office you preferre.
—JOHN DONNE, "TO THE COUNTESSE OF HUNTINGDON" (1608)

Man is the will, and woman the sentiment. In this ship of humanity, will is the rudder, and sentiment the sail; when woman affects to steer, the rudder is only a masked sail.
—RALPH WALDO EMERSON, "WOMAN" (ca. 1850)

Women are to have fun with. In politics I prefer not to see a woman. Instead of getting all worked up, they should stay as they are—like flowers.

—LECH WALESA, POLISH POLITICAL LEADER (1981)

■ *The Scottish reformer John Knox's* **First Blast of the Trumpet Against the Monstrous Regiment of Women** *(1558) remained popular for more than 350 years. It was widely used as ammunition in the woman suffrage debate.*

Promoting a woman to regiment [rule], superioritie, dominion, or empire above any realme, nation or citie is repugnant to nature, contumelie to God, a thing most contrarious to His revealed will and approved ordinance; and finallie it is the subversion of good order, of all equitie and justice. . . . Their sight in civile regiment is but blindnes: their strength, weaknes: their counsel, foolishnes: and judgement, phrenesie, if it be rightly considered. . . . The same [God] that hath denied power to the hand to speake, to the bely to heare, and to the feet to see, hath denied to women power to commande man, and hath taken away wisdome to consider, and providence to foresee the things, that be profitable to the common welth: yea finallie he hath denied to her in any case to be head to man.

—JOHN KNOX, *THE FIRST BLAST OF THE TRUMPET AGAINST
THE MONSTROUS REGIMENT OF WOMEN* (1558)

For a woman to rule is as for a hen to crow in the mornings.

—JAPANESE PROVERB

Where woman reigns war rages.

—SICILIAN PROVERB

A woman could never be president. A candidate must be thirty-five or over—and where are you going to find a woman who will admit she's over thirty-five?

—AMERICAN JOKE (ca. 1950)

■ *Let us solicit the opinions of some American presidents:*

The appointment of a woman to office is an innovation for which the public is not prepared, nor am I.

—THOMAS JEFFERSON, LETTER TO ALBERT GALLATIN (JANUARY 1807)

Depend upon it, We know better than to repeal our Masculine systems. . . . We have only the Name of Masters, and rather than give up this, which would compleatly subject Us to the Despotism of the Peticoat, I hope General Washington, and all our brave Heroes would fight.

—JOHN ADAMS, LETTER TO ABIGAIL ADAMS (APRIL 14, 1776)

■ *President Grover Cleveland comforts us by reminding us yet again that any political or economic inequities women may suffer were ordained by God. From "Would Woman Suffrage be Unwise?" (1905):*

It is a mistake to suppose that any human reasoning or argument is needful or adequate to the assignment of the relative positions to be assumed by man and woman in working out the problems of civilization. This was done long ago by a higher intelligence than ours. I believe that trust in Divine wisdom . . . will enable dutiful men and women to know the places assigned to them, and will incite them to act well their parts in the sight of God. . . .

Legislators should never neglect the dictates of chivalry in their treatment of woman; but this does not demand that a smirking appearance of acquiescence should conceal or smother a thoughtful lawmaker's intelligent disapproval of female suffrage. It is one of the chief charms of women that they are not especially amenable to argument; but that is not a reason why, when they demand the ballot as an inherent right, they should not be reminded that suffrage is a privilege which attaches neither to man nor to woman by nature. . . .

I have sometimes wondered if the really good women who are inclined to approve this doctrine of female suffrage are not deluding themselves with purely sentimental views of the subject. Have they not in some way allowed the idea to gain a place in their minds that if the suffrage were accorded to women it would be the pure, the honest, the intelligent and the patriotic of the sex who would avail themselves of it? . . . Even if every woman in the land should exercise the suffrage, the votes of the thoughtful and conscientious would almost certainly be largely outweighed by those of the disreputable, the ignorant, the thoughtless, the purchased and the coerced. . . .

This phase of the suffrage question cannot better be presented than in the following words of another: "Women change politics less than politics change women."

—PRESIDENT GROVER CLEVELAND, "WOULD WOMAN SUFFRAGE BE UNWISE?" (1905)

■ *Yet another example of impeccable male logic, from "Woman's Rights," a popular nineteenth-century antisuffrage tract:*

At one time the women of Rome became so discouraged and downhearted with their condition, that they committed suicide to such an extent that the Senate, alarmed, passed a decree that all who should henceforth commit suicide should have their bodies exposed, *naked,* in the streets. The instincts of modesty came to woman's aid, and there were no more suicides. On the true instincts of the sex I rely, while I speak to the women of my generation kindly, faithfully, plainly, calmly, and decidedly. . . .

The demand is . . . that [women] shall be educated as [man] is, enter the same pursuits that he does, receive the same wages, occupy the same posts and professions, wield the same influence, and, in a word, be independent of man. . . .

"Why, then," my lady reader will say, "*why* can't we be independent of man?" for this is the gist of the whole subject. I reply, you can't, for two reasons: first, God never designed you should, and secondly, your own deep instincts are in the way. . . .

A great hue and cry is set up about the right of women to vote, and the cruelty of denying them this right. Plainly this is merely a civil and not a natural right. Minors, foreigners, and idiots are denied it. . . .

[In the matter of wages] we can't have justice. . . . But bear in mind that God has put the labor and the duty on men to support the families. . . . Is it then so very unjust that woman, who has no such responsibility, does not receive so high wages? . . .

O woman! your worst enemy is he . . . who would cruelly lift you out of your spheres and try to reverse the very laws of God . . . when your only safety and happiness is in patiently, lovingly, and faithfully performing the duties and enacting the relations of your own sphere.

—REV. JOHN TODD, "WOMAN'S RIGHTS" (1867)

■ *The discerning reader will note that what may appear to be a political argument is actually an economic one. Such is the subtlety of our Great Men.*

An Equal Rights Amendment to the U.S. Constitution has been introduced, and defeated, in every Congress since 1923. The Amendment states: "Equality of rights under the law shall not be denied or abridged by the United States or by any State on account of sex." Some arguments against the Equal Rights Amendment:

Ever since Adam gave up his rib to make a woman, throughout the ages we have learned that physical, emotional, psychological and social differences exist and dare not be disregarded. . . .

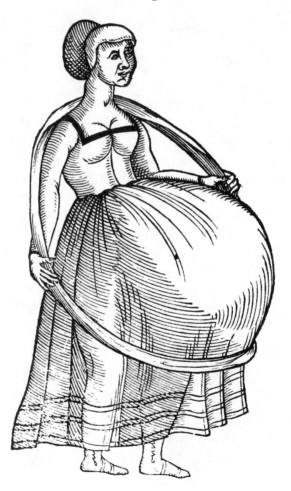

The equal rights amendment may require changes in the traditional roles of the husband as breadwinner and the wife as householder. . . . The intrusion of the hand of government into the delicate personal relationship of a husband and wife . . . would bring grief untold.

—REPRESENTATIVE EMANUEL CELLER, *CONGRESSIONAL RECORD*, 116TH CONGRESS (1970)

When He created them, God made physiological and functional differences between men and women. These differences . . . constitute earth's important reality. Without them human life could not exist.

For this reason, any country which ignores these differences when it fashions its institutions and makes its law is woefully lacking in rationality.

—SENATOR SAM J. ERVIN, JR., *CONGRESSIONAL RECORD*, 116TH CONGRESS (1970)

There are many laws specifically protecting working women. . . . These laws would be thrown into confusion. So would a great body of law governing divorce, child support, custody, alimony, the age at which a woman reaches her majority, and a widow's rights in her husband's estate.

—EDITORIAL, *THE NEW YORK TIMES* (AUGUST 12, 1970)

Women are not equal and never could be.

—CHARLES BRONSON, AMERICAN ACTOR (1977)

The truth is that women's income, on average, will always be a fraction of men's, so long as America remains free.

—PATRICK BUCHANAN, AMERICAN POLITICAL COLUMNIST (1984)

■ *In short, to institutionalize equal rights for women would cause unacceptable inconvenience to men.*

While real-life women will no doubt continue to vex their masters by demanding equality, women in literature are sometimes more cooperative.

I am asham'd that women are so simple
To offer war, where they should kneel for peace,
Or seek for rule, supremacy, and sway,
When they are bound to serve, love and obey.
Why are our bodies soft, and weak, and smooth,
Unapt to toil and trouble in the world,
But that our soft conditions and our hearts
Should well agree with our external parts?
—KATHERINA IN WILLIAM SHAKESPEARE, *THE TAMING OF THE SHREW* (1623)

Wommen are born to thraldom and penance
And to ben under mannes governance.
—THE SAINTLY CONSTANCE IN "THE MAN OF LAW'S TALE" IN GEOFFREY CHAUCER,
CANTERBURY TALES (1369)

Educating the Female

Education is the key to the peaceful domestication of the female. By properly educating her to the role that accords with her approved character and destiny, Man may eliminate the need for force in keeping woman to her proper sphere.

To help us determine those female qualities worthy of cultivation, let us first consider those that are not.

Very little wit is valued in a woman, as we are pleased with the few words of a parrot.

—JONATHAN SWIFT (ca. 1730)

Men hate learned women.

—ALFRED, LORD TENNYSON, "THE PRINCESS" (1847)

The brain-women never interest us like the heart-women; white roses please less than red.

—OLIVER WENDELL HOLMES, *THE PROFESSOR AT THE BREAKFAST-TABLE* (1859)

Brains are never a handicap to a girl if she hides them under a see-through blouse.

—BOBBY VINTON, AMERICAN ENTERTAINER (1978)

Thought does not become a young woman.

> —MRS. MALAPROP IN RICHARD BRINSLEY SHERIDAN, *THE RIVALS* (1775)

Eloquence in women shouldn't be praised; it is more fitting for them to lisp and stammer. This is more becoming to them.

> —MARTIN LUTHER, *TABLE TALK* (1538)

Ladies supreme among amusements reign;
By nature born to soothe and entertain.
Their prudence in a share of folly lies:
Why will they be so weak, as to be wise?

> —EDWARD YOUNG, *THE UNIVERSAL PASSION* (1725–28)

A wise woman is twice a fool.

> —MEDIEVAL LATIN PROVERB

No women should have a memory. Memory in a woman is the beginning of dowdiness.

> —LORD ILLINGWORTH IN OSCAR WILDE, *A WOMAN OF NO IMPORTANCE* (1893)

If we wish a woman to fulfill her task of motherhood fully, she cannot possess a masculine brain. If the feminine abilities were developed to the same degree as those of the male, woman's maternal organs would suffer and we should have a repulsive and useless hybrid.

> —P. J. MOEBIUS, *CONCERNING THE PHYSIOLOGICAL INTELLECTUAL FEEBLENESS OF WOMEN*
> (1907)

A woman who has a head full of Greek . . . or carries on fundamental controversies about mechanics, might as well have a beard.

> —IMMANUEL KANT, *OBSERVATIONS ON THE FEELING OF THE BEAUTIFUL AND THE SUBLIME*
> (1764)

I'd as lief your little head
Should be cumbered up with lead
As with learning, live or dead,
  Or with brains.

—RICHARD MONCKTON MILNES, "TO DORIS" (ca. 1870)

■ *On a more positive note, let us explore some desirable female qualities.*

I am very fond of the company of ladies. I like their beauty, I like their delicacy, I like their vivacity, and I like their *silence.*
—SAMUEL JOHNSON (ca. 1760)

Silence gives the proper grace to women.
—TEKMESSA IN SOPHOCLES, *AJAX* (ca. 450 B.C.)

Let the woman learn in silence with all subjection. But I suffer not a woman to teach, nor to usurp authority over the man, but to be in silence. For Adam was first formed, then Eve. And Adam was not deceived, but the woman being deceived was in the transgression.

Notwithstanding she shall be saved in childbearing, if they continue in faith and charity and holiness with sobriety.
—NEW TESTAMENT, 1 TIMOTHY 2:11–15 (ca. A.D. 50)

"God is thy law, thou mine: to know no more
Is woman's happiest knowledge and her praise."
—EVE, TO ADAM, IN JOHN MILTON, *PARADISE LOST* (1665)

Her faith is fixt and cannot move,
    She darkly feels him great and wise,
    She dwells on him with faithful eyes,
"I cannot understand; I love."
—ALFRED, LORD TENNYSON, *IN MEMORIAM* (1850)

■ *Consider the purpose of female education.*

[In the education of girls] the main stress should be put on physical training, and only after this on the promotion of spiritual and last of all, the intellectual values. The *goal* of female education has invariably to be the future mother.

—ADOLF HITLER, *MEIN KAMPF* (1927)

I want to remind young women that motherhood is the vocation of women. . . . It is women's eternal vocation.

—POPE JOHN PAUL II, AT HIS WEEKLY GENERAL AUDIENCE (JANUARY 10, 1979)

The glory of a man is knowledge, but the glory of a woman is to renounce knowledge.

—CHINESE PROVERB

It would be preposterously naive to suggest that a B.A. can be made as attractive to girls as a marriage license.

—DR. GRAYSON KIRK, PRESIDENT OF COLUMBIA UNIVERSITY (1967)

■ *Should women learn to read and write at all?*

If you have a female child, set her to sewing and not to reading. . . . Teach her to be useful in the house, to make bread, to clean chickens, to sift, cook, launder and spin . . . to put new feet into socks, and so on; then, when you marry her off, she won't seem an ignoramus.

—PAOLO DA CERTALDO, *HANDBOOK OF GOOD CUSTOMS* (ca. 1360)

■ *From a professional educator:*

Not only the probability and desirability of marriage and the training of children as an essential feature of women's career but also the restriction of women to the mediocre grades of ability and achievement should be reckoned with by our educational systems. The education of women for such professions as administration, statesmanship, philosophy, or scientific research, where a few very gifted individuals are what society requires, is far less needed than education for such professions as nursing, teaching, medicine, or architecture, where the average level is essential.

—DR. EDWARD L. THORNDIKE, "SEX IN EDUCATION" (1906)

■ *The consequences of excessive female education can be painful indeed. An anecdote from the Journal of the first Governor of Massachusetts:*

Mr. Hopkins, the governour of Hartford upon Connecticut, came to Boston and brought his wife with him (a godly young woman, and of special parts), who had fallen into a sad infirmity, the loss of her understanding and reason, which had been growing on her divers years, by occasion of her giving herself wholly to reading and writing, and had written many books.

Her husband, being very loving and tender of her, was loathe to grieve her; but he saw his error, when it was too late.

For if she had attended her household affairs, and such things as belong to women, and not gone out of her way and calling to meddle in such things as are proper for men, whose minds are stronger, etc., she had kept her wits, and might have improved them usefully and honorably in the place God set for her.

—GOVERNOR JOHN WINTHROP, WINTHROP'S JOURNAL (1645)

Under our lamentable system of modern education, woman is not taught the defects and limitations of the female mind . . . the failure to recognize that man is the master, and why he is the master, lies at the root of the suffrage problem. . . . Man is the natural master of woman for three reasons: first, his superior physical force, the power of compulsion upon which all government is based; second, his intellectual superiority; and third, his superior money-earning capacity.

—SIR AMROTH EDWARD WRIGHT, *THE UNEXPURGATED CASE AGAINST WOMAN SUFFRAGE*
(1913)

The best schools and colleges are open to such of them as desire a higher education until a new danger now threatens us of creating in them a distaste for manual labor, which has almost removed the native American girl from her natural vocation of housekeeping.

—JUSTICE HENRY BILLINGS BROWN, "WOMAN SUFFRAGE" (1910)

■ *Thus it is easy to see why the education of females runs contrary to the forward march of civilization.*

Educating a woman is like pouring honey over a fine Swiss watch. It stops working.

—KURT VONNEGUT, INTERVIEW (1985)

Educating a woman is like handing a knife to a monkey.

—HINDU PROVERB

Who teaches a woman letters feeds more poison to a frightful asp.

—MENANDER (ca. 300 B.C.)

For a woman to study [the Vedas] indicates confusion in the realm.

—THE *MAHABHARATA* (ca. 300 B.C.)

The words of the Torah should be burned rather than taught to women.

—TALMUD, SOTAH 3:4 (ca. A.D. 150)

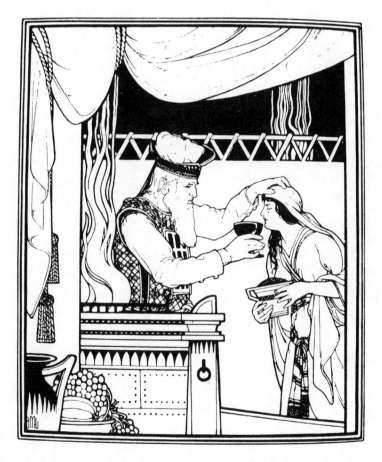

■ *In this direction lie the happiness and convenience of men.*

A man . . . is always happiest with a woman who is deferentially his inferior. It is the equality of woman to man in the Anglo-Saxon countries . . . that is the cause of man's frequent dissatisfaction with his married lot and of the consequent alarming increase in the divorce rate. A marriage in which the wife knows the difference between a sonata and a *Geburtsleid* . . . and the batting average of Babe Ruth, is always on its way to consult a shyster lawyer. The most successful marriage is ever the one in which the wife believes the husband to be a compendium of all the refinements of wisdom and understanding, however an ass the husband may really be.

—GEORGE JEAN NATHAN (ca. 1929)

But—Oh! ye lords of ladies intellectual,
Inform us truly, have they not hen-peck'd you all?

—LORD BYRON, DON JUAN (1818)

A whistling woman and a crowing hen
Is neither fit for God nor men.

—ENGLISH, HINDU, AND SPANISH PROVERBS

Let your women keep silence in the churches: for it is not permitted them to speak; but they are commanded to be under obedience, as also saith the law.

—NEW TESTAMENT, 1 CORINTHIANS 14:34 (ca. A.D. 50)

■ *As for preaching women:*

Complaint was made to William Pickering, then Mayor, that two women were preaching. . . . He asked their names [and] their hus-

bands' names. They told him: they had no husband but Jesus Christ and He sent them. Upon this the Mayor grew angry, called them whores and issued his warrant to the constable to whip them at the Market-Cross until the blood ran down their bodies. . . . So they were led to the Market-Cross. . . . The executioner . . . stripped them naked to the waist, put their arms into the whipping-post and executed the Mayor's warrant . . . so that their flesh was miserably cut and torn.
—JOSEPH BESSE, *A COLLECTION OF THE SUFFERINGS OF THE PEOPLE CALLED QUAKERS* (1753)

A woman's preaching is like a dog's walking on his hind legs. It is not done well; but you are surprised to find it done at all.
—SAMUEL JOHNSON (JULY 31, 1763)

■ *Finally, let us look at the methodology of female education and the recommendations of experts for the correct cultivation of feminine virtues.*

Women, destined to be obedient, ought to be disciplined early to bear wrongs without murmuring.
—H. H. KAMES, *LOOSE HINTS UPON EDUCATION* (1781)

Some say that learning seems not to be the business of women. I say that . . . control of the mind is of the utmost importance to women, and it would be a great mistake to say that it is not their business. The outward manner and temper of women is rooted in the negative (yin) power, and so temperamentally women are apt to be sensitive, petty, narrow, and jaundiced. As they live confined to their homes day in and day out, theirs is a very private life and their vision is quite limited. Consequently, among women compassion and honesty are rare indeed. That is why Buddhism says that women are particularly sinful and have the greatest difficulty in attaining Buddhahood. Thus women are in special need of mental discipline.

—NAKAE TŌJU, *TŌJU SENSEI ZENSHŪ* (JAPANESE, ca. 1640)

False also and harmful to Christian education is the so-called method of "coeducation." . . . There is not in nature itself, which fashions the two quite different in organism, in temperament, in abilities, anything to suggest that there can be or ought to be promiscuity, and much less equality, in the training of the two sexes.

—POPE PIUS XI, ENCYCLICAL *DIVINI ILLIUS MAGISTRI* (1929)

■ *Principles for the education of girls, from the great philosopher of the French Enlightenment, Jean-Jacques Rousseau:*

A perfect man and a perfect woman should no more resemble each other in mind than in countenance. . . . It is the part of one to be active and strong, and of the other to be passive and weak. Accept this principle and it follows in the second place that woman is intended to please man. . . .

For this reason [women's] education must be wholly directed to their relations with men. To give them pleasure, to be useful to them, to win their love and esteem, to train them in their childhood, to care for them when they grow up . . .: these are the tasks of women in all times for which they should be trained from childhood. . . .

In boys the object of physical training is the development of strength, in girls the development of graces. . . . Boys like movement and noise: their toys are drums, tops and go-carts. Girls would rather have things that look well and serve for adornment: mirrors, jewels, dress materials and most of all dolls. . . . Here the girl's liking is plainly directed towards her lifework. . . . The time will come when she will be her own doll. . . . As a matter of fact nearly all little girls greatly dislike learning to read and write but they are always willing to learn to use the needle. They imagine themselves grown up and think happily of the time when they will be using their talents in adorning themselves. . . .

Girls are generally more docile than boys and in any case have more need to be brought under authority. . . . This hardship, if it be a hardship, is inseparable from their sex. All their life they will be under the hard, unceasing constraints of the proprieties. They must be disciplined to endure them . . . for dependence is a state natural to women, and girls realise that they are made for obedience. . . .

The first and most important quality of a woman is sweetness. . . . She must learn to submit uncomplainingly to unjust treatment and marital wrongs. . . .

Girls should always be submissive, but mothers should not always be inexorable. . . . Indeed I should not be sorry if sometimes she were allowed to exercise a little cunning, not to elude punishment but to escape having to obey. Guile is a natural gift of her sex; and being convinced that all natural dispositions are good and right in themselves I think that this one should be cultivated like the rest. The characteristic cunning with which women are endowed is an equitable compensation for their lesser strength.

—JEAN JACQUES ROUSSEAU, *ÉMILE, OR ON EDUCATION* (1762)

■ *The wise husband will be circumspect in what he imparts to his wife.*

Though you love your wife, do not tell her all you know; tell her some trifle, and conceal the rest.
—AGAMEMNON IN HOMER, *ODYSSEY* (ca. 800 B.C.)

He that tells his wife news is but newly married.
—ENGLISH PROVERB (17TH CENTURY)

He knows little who will tell his wife all he knows.
—THOMAS FULLER, "THE GOOD HUSBAND" (1642)

Satisfy a dog with a bone and a woman with a lie.
—BASQUE PROVERB

Be to her Virtues very kind;
Be to her Faults a little blind;
Let all her Ways be unconfin'd;
And clap your PADLOCK—on her Mind.
—BICKERSTAFFE IN MATTHEW PRIOR, *AN ENGLISH PADLOCK* (1704)

■ *To go right to the heart of the matter:*

I like them fluffy—I know it's bad taste—
With fluffy soft looks and a flower at the waist,
With golden hair flying, like mist round the moon
And lips that seem sighing, "You must kiss me soon,"
    Not huffy, or stuffy, not tiny or tall,
    But fluffy, just fluffy, with no brains at all.
—SIR ALAN PATRICK HERBERT, "I LIKE THEM FLUFFY" (1927)

13

Woman's
Contemptible Weaknesses

If the programs outlined above have been successful—if, through the combined application of law, religion, custom, the whip, and persistent education, the dangerous alien being is transformed into a harmless pussycat—then Man's tireless struggle to uphold his supremacy will not have been in vain.

Let us proceed to an examination of what we may call the female intellect.

Women have long hair and short brains.
—ESTONIAN, KALMUK, LIVONIAN, RUSSIAN, SLOVENIAN, AND SWEDISH PROVERBS

When an ass climbeth a ladder you may find wisdom in women.
—ENGLISH PROVERB (18TH CENTURY)

A woman cuts her wisdom teeth when she is dead.
—ROMANIAN PROVERB

All the characteristics of woman's body and mind . . . are dependent on the activity of her ovaries.
—RUDOLF VIRCHOW, GERMAN BIOLOGIST (ca. 1880)

Woman's reason is in the milk of her breasts.
—GEORGE MEREDITH, *THE ORDEAL OF RICHARD FEVEREL* (1859)

A woman's breast is the organ with which she is able to express herself
most intelligently. It is her language and poetry, her history and her
music, her purity and her desire. . . . The bosom is the central organ
of all female ideas, wishes, and moods.

—LEO BERG, *THE SEXUAL PROBLEM IN ART AND LIFE* (1891)

Like most women, my wife thinks with her glands, not with her head.

—SENATOR MARK HATFIELD (1974)

■ *From* **Man Superior to Woman,** *an eighteenth-century best-seller
by an Anonymous Gentleman, "Containing a plain Confutation of the
fallacious Arguments of Sophia, in her late Treatise intitled,* **Woman
not inferior to Man***":*

Whether Women *are equal to* Men *in their intellectual Capacity, or not*
If the Business of the Mind were nothing more than to contrive a
Dress; to invent a new Fashion; to set off a bad Face; to heighten the
Charms of a good one; to understand the Economy of a Tea-Table; to
manage an Intrigue; to conduct a Game at *Quadrille,* and to lay out new
Plans of Pleasure, Pride and Luxury; then *Women* must be own'd to
have a Capacity not only *equal* but even superior to us. But as the
Understanding of *Man* has infinitely higher Objects to employ its Spec-
ulations on, Objects beyond the very Aim of the ablest *Women;* their
intellectual Faculties are so evidently inferior to his, that I should think
it an Impertinence in me to take up any Time to prove it, if my fair
Adversary was not *Woman* enough to call so palpable a Truth in Question.

Need we look any farther than their soft, simpering, silly Faces to
fathom the perceptible Depth of their Understandings? View the whole
Sex round:

Eternal Smiles their Emptiness betray
As shallow Streams run dimpling all the way.
(POPE)

A thoughtless Stare, a wild Vivacity, a sleepy Pertness, giddy Gravity, or some such other Sense-defying Look betrays, in all, the narrow Space between the Surface and the Centre of their mimic Wit. . . .

In Fact, what is all their Discourse but *Froth?* What inspires it but Venom? In what does their Sprightliness appear, but in empty Puns, Conundrums, Rebukes, trifling Politics or mischievous Lies? They, who shine most among them, are such as have nothing to entertain you with but Scandal, Indecency, Hypocrisy, or Impiety. What is their Wit but a mere See-Saw from one Inconsistency to another? Their Conversation is ever screw'd up to Bombast, when it should be familiar; or sunk into Meanness, when the Subject they presume to meddle with is sublime. Where they should be silent, they are as forward to prate, as they are remiss in speaking on proper Occasions. . . .

How ill-bestow'd then on these fantastic Things is the Beauty we admire in them! And if it was bestow'd on them by Nature to decoy us into a Commerce with them, for the Benefit of Propagation; must it not still shock our Reason when we consider it accompanied only with Parts which we can reap no Benefit from, nor place any Confidence in? And what Assistance can we hope from their false Wit, as groveling as the Pride it inspires them with?

—ANON., *MAN SUPERIOR TO WOMAN* (1739)

With women one should never venture to joke.
—MEPHISTOPHELES IN JOHANN WOLFGANG VON GOETHE, *FAUST* (1808–32)

Q: How many feminists does it take to change a light bulb?
A: That's not funny!

—AMERICAN JOKE (ca. 1985)

■ *The primary deficiency of the female intellect can be seen in its devotion to the pointless pastime of pleasing men.*

Women's thoughts are ever turned upon appearing amiable to the other sex; they talk and move and smile with a design upon us; every feature of their faces, every part of their dress, is filled with snares and allurements. There would be no such animals as prudes or coquettes in the world were there not such an animal as man.

—JOSEPH ADDISON, *THE SPECTATOR* (1711–12)

Women are much more like each other than men: they have, in truth, but two passions, vanity and love; these are their universal characteristics.

—LORD CHESTERFIELD, LETTER TO HIS SON (DECEMBER 19, 1749)

Man's love is of man's life a thing apart,
'Tis a woman's whole existence.

—LORD BYRON, *DON JUAN* (1818)

Once a woman has given you her heart, you can never get rid of the rest of her.

—LOVELESS IN SIR JOHN VANBRUGH, *THE RELAPSE* (1696)

In general, it is probable that the consciousness of how one stands with other people occupies a relatively larger and larger part of the mind, the lower one goes in the scale of culture. Woman's intuition, so fine in the sphere of personal relations, is seldom first-rate in the way of mechanics. All boys teach themselves how a clock goes; few girls. Hence Dr. Whately's jest, "Woman is the unreasoning animal, and pokes the fire from the top."

—WILLIAM JAMES, *PRINCIPLES OF PSYCHOLOGY* (1890)

■ *Not everyone agrees that women's devotion to men is all it should be.*

Women have many faults, but the worst of them all is that they are too pleased with themselves and take too little pains to please the men.

—ADELPHASIUM IN PLAUTUS, *POENULUS* (191 B.C.)

■ *The vanity of women has frequently been commented upon, both indulgently and otherwise.*

For there was never yet fair woman but she made mouths in a glass.

—FOOL IN WILLIAM SHAKESPEARE, *KING LEAR* (1606)

The things for which a woman yearns are adornments.

—TALMUD, KETUBOT 65 (ca. A.D. 250)

If our faith here on earth were on the same scale as the wages awaiting us in heaven, not one of you, my dear sisters, once she had come to know God and to recognize her condition as a woman, would lust after pleasure or finery. Rather would she go weeping like Eve, mourning and repentant, in rags and in ashes, trying to expiate by her meanness of appearance the disgrace of that first sin and the odium of human perdition.

Do you not know that you are each an Eve? God's judgment upon your sex endures even today, and with it endures the weight of your guilt. *You* are the devil's gateway: *You* are the unsealer of the tree: *You* are the first deserter of the divine law: *You* are she who persuaded him whom the devil was not brave enough to attack. How easily you destroyed God's image: man. On account of *your* reward—that is, death—even the Son of God had to die.

—TERTULLIAN, ON THE APPAREL OF WOMEN (ca. A.D. 200)

As Divines say, that some People take more pains to be Damned, than it would cost them to be Saved, so your Sex employs more thought, memory, and application to be Fools, than would serve to make them wise and useful. When I reflect on this, I cannot conceive you to be Human Creatures, but a sort of Species hardly a degree above a Monkey; who has more diverting Tricks than any of you; is an Animal less mischievous and expensive, might in time be a tolerable Critick in Velvet and Brocade, and for ought I know wou'd equally become them.

—JONATHAN SWIFT, "A LETTER TO A YOUNG LADY ON HER MARRIAGE" (1727)

A beautiful woman who gives pleasure to men serves only to frighten the fish when she jumps into the water.

—CHUANG-TSU (ca. 300 B.C.)

■ *Female wiles may appear frivolous, but they contain economic implications of which alert men should be aware.*

All said, the female who keeps her cunt hymenized and under seal among the well-to-do classes, only does so that she may get a higher price for it, either in money or position. She sometimes never attains either, and mostly has to wait long for it . . . languishing for want of a prick and spermatic lubrication, which is health-giving to a female. . . .

Women are all bought in the market—from the whore to the Princess. The price alone is different, and the highest price, in money or rank, obtains the woman.

—ANON., *MY SECRET LIFE* (1890)

Maidens, like moths, are ever caught by glare,
And Mammon wins his way where seraphs might despair.

—LORD BYRON, *CHILDE HAROLD'S PILGRIMAGE* (1812)

Hares are caught with dogs, fools with flattery, and women with money.

—GERMAN PROVERB

What female heart can gold despise?
What cat's averse to fish?

—THOMAS GRAY, "ON THE DEATH OF A FAVOURITE CAT" (ca. 1750)

A woman's brain is divided into two parts—dollars and cents.

—AMERICAN JOKE (ca. 1950)

■ *How characteristic of perfidious woman to be economically motivated!*

What do women need money for?

—MICK JAGGER, BRITISH ROCK STAR (1978)

Do not let a flaunting woman coax and cozen and deceive you: she is after your barn.

—HESIOD, *WORKS AND DAYS* (ca. 800 B.C.)

Dumb jewels often in their silent kind
More than quick words do move a woman's mind.

—VALENTINE IN WILLIAM SHAKESPEARE, *TWO GENTLEMEN OF VERONA* (1592)

■ *The "penis envy" theory, continuing from page 87 above, concludes by drawing the connection between woman's physical vanity and her mental aberrations.*

The effect of penis-envy has a share, further, in the physical vanity of women, since they are bound to value their charms more highly as a late compensation for their original sexual inferiority. Shame, which is considered to be a feminine characteristic *par excellence* . . . has as its purpose, we believe, concealment of genital deficiency. . . . It seems that women have made few contributions to . . . civilization; there is, however, one technique which they have invented—that of plaiting

and weaving. If that is so, we should be tempted to guess the unconscious motive for the achievement. Nature herself would seem to have given the model which this achievement imitates by causing the growth at maturity of the pubic hair that conceals the genitals. . . .

A man of about thirty strikes us as a youthful, somewhat unformed individual. . . . A woman of the same age, however, often frightens us by her psychical rigidity and unchangeability. . . . There are no paths open to further development; it is as though the whole process had already run its course and remains thenceforward insusceptible to influence—as though, indeed, the difficult development which leads to femininity had exhausted the possibilities of the person concerned.

—SIGMUND FREUD, "FEMININITY" (1933)

The average woman's judgment is never as good as the average man's —and when they pass the age of forty, their ability to reason seems to deteriorate quite rapidly.

—PAUL LAMET, FRENCH PSYCHOLOGIST (1990)

Time and circumstance, which enlarge the views of most men, narrow the views of women almost invariably.

—THOMAS HARDY, *JUDE THE OBSCURE* (1895)

■ *One wonders why this should be. Perhaps it has something to do with evolution.*

Woman seems to differ from man in mental disposition. . . . It is generally admitted that with woman the powers of intuition, of rapid perception, and perhaps of imitation, are more strongly marked than in man; but some, at least, of these faculties are characteristic of the lower races, and therefore of a past and lower state of civilisation.

The chief distinction in the intellectual powers of the two sexes is shewn by man attaining to a higher eminence, in whatever he takes up, than woman can attain—whether requiring deep thought, reason, or imagination, or merly the use of the senses and hands.

Although men do not now fight for the sake of obtaining wives, and this form of selection has passed away, yet they generally have to undergo, during manhood, a severe struggle in order to maintain themselves and their families; and this will tend to keep up or even increase their mental powers, and, as a consequence, the present inequality between the sexes.

—CHARLES DARWIN, *THE DESCENT OF MAN, AND SELECTION IN RELATION TO SEX* (1871)

■ *This helps to explain why there has never been, and never can be, a female genius.*

For a penetrating analysis of this phenomenon, let us turn to an expert: the German philosopher Otto Weininger, who wrote extensively on the subject of genius. Tragically, Weininger committed suicide at the age of twenty-three when the world failed to acknowledge his gifts. From his masterpiece, **Sex and Character** *(1903):*

In such a being as the absolute female there are no logical and ethical phenomena, and, therefore, the ground for the assumption of a soul is absent. The absolute female knows neither the logical nor the moral imperative, and the words law and duty, duty towards herself, are words which are least familiar to her. . . .

The Chinese from time immemorial have denied that women possess a personal soul. If a Chinese man is asked how many children he has, he counts only the boys, and will say none if he has only daughters. Mahomet excluded women from Paradise for the same reason, and on this view depends the degraded position of women in Oriental countries.

Amongst the philosophers, the opinions of Aristotle must first be considered. . . . Amongst the fathers of the Church, Tertullian and Origen certainly had a very low opinion of woman, and St. Augustine, except for his relations with his mother, . . . seems to have shared their view. . . . In recent years Henrik Ibsen . . . and August Strindberg have given utterance to this view. . . .

Since the soul of man is the microcosm, and great men are those who live entirely in and through their souls, the whole universe thus having its being in them, the female must be described as absolutely without the quality of genius. . . . There is no female genius, and there never has been one . . . *and there never can be one.* Those who are in favor of laxity in these matters, and are anxious to extend and enlarge the idea of genius in order to make it possible to include women, would simply by such action destroy the concept of genius. . . . How could a soulless being possess genius? The possession of genius is identical with profundity; and if any one were to try to combine woman and profundity as subject and predicate, he would be contradicted on all sides. A female genius is a contradiction in terms, for genius is simply intensified, perfectly developed, universally conscious maleness.

—OTTO WEININGER, *SEX AND CHARACTER* (1903)

■ *Others agree.*

Women have, in general, no love of any art; they have no proper knowledge of any; and they have no genius.

—JEAN JACQUES ROUSSEAU, "LETTRE À D'ALEMBERT" (1758)

No woman ever wrote a really good book.

—LORD MELBOURNE, TO QUEEN VICTORIA (1838)

There's no music when a woman is in the concert.

—MATHEO IN THOMAS DEKKER, *THE HONEST WHORE* (1604)

The best players are men. . . . It is strange for me to see women players. I like the uniformity of one sex in the orchestra.

—ARTHUR FIEDLER, CONDUCTOR, THE BOSTON POPS SYMPHONY ORCHESTRA (1978)

Would any link be missing from the whole chain of science and art, if woman, if woman's work, were excluded from it? Let us acknowledge the exception—it proves the rule—that woman is capable of perfection in everything which does not constitute a work: in letters, in memoirs, in the most intricate handiwork—in short, everything which is not a craft; and precisely because in the things mentioned woman perfects herself, because in them she obeys the only artistic impulse in her nature, which is to captivate.

—FRIEDRICH NIETZSCHE, *THE WILL TO POWER* (1888)

■ *What is the ultimate source of male achievement?*

The undoubted superiority of the male sex in intellectual and creative achievement is related to their greater endowment of aggression. . . . Even when women have been given the opportunity to cultivate the arts and sciences, remarkably few have produced original works of outstanding quality.

—ANTHONY STORR, *HUMAN AGGRESSION* (1968)

Women by their nature are not exceptional chess players. They are not great fighters.

—GARY KASPAROV, WORLD CHESS CHAMPION (1990)

■ *There are philosophical reasons why the possession of a superior intellect is beyond the reach of women.*

The man has his real essential life in the state, in sciences and the like, in battle and in struggle with the outside world and with himself. . . . The woman has her true substantive place in the family. . . .

Women are, of course, capable of being educated, but their minds are not really adaptable to the higher sciences, philosophy, or certain of the creative arts. These demand a faculty for the universal. Women may have good ideas, good taste, and elegance, but they lack the talent for the ideal.

Men and women differ much as animals and plants do. Men and animals correspond, as do women and plants, for women develop more placidly and always retain the formless indeterminate unity of feeling and sentiment. When women have control over the government, the state is plunged into peril, for they do not act according to the standards of universality, but are influenced by random inclinations and opinions.

—GEORG WILHELM FRIEDRICH HEGEL, *PHILOSOPHY OF RIGHT* (1821)

Intellectually, a certain inferiority of the female sex can hardly be denied. . . . Women are intellectually more desultory and volatile than men; they are more occupied with particular instances than with general principles; they judge rather by intuitive perceptions than by deliberate reasoning.

—WILLIAM EDWARD HARTPOLE LECKY, *HISTORY OF EUROPEAN MORALS* (1869)

The king then asked the next [philosopher], How he could live amicably with his wife? And he answered, "By recognizing that womankind are by nature headstrong and energetic in the pursuit of their own desires, and subject to sudden changes of opinion through fallacious reasoning, and their nature is essentially weak. It is necessary to deal wisely with them and not to provoke strife. . . ." The king expressed his agreement.

—PSEUDEPIGRAPHA, *LETTER OF ARISTAEAS* (ca. 100 B.C.)

■ *Woman's chief mental mode is romantic vacillation.*

La donna è mobile
Qual piuma al vento.
(Woman is fickle as a feather in the wind.)

—F. M. PIAVE, *RIGOLETTO* (1851)

Elle flotte, elle hésite; en un mot, elle est femme.
(She wavers, she hesitates; in a word, she is woman.)

—MATHAN IN JEAN RACINE, *ATHALIE* (1691)

Varium et mutabile semper femina.
(Woman is always a fickle and changeable thing.)

—LATIN PROVERB, IN VERGIL, *AENEID* (ca. 25 B.C.)

Les femmes ont toujours quelque arrière pensée.
(Women always have second thoughts.)

—FRENCH, JAPANESE, AND TAMIL PROVERBS

■ *So what must Man conclude?*

This record will forever stand,
"Woman, thy vows are traced in sand."

—LORD BYRON, "TO WOMAN" (1806)

Woman's love is writ in water,
Woman's faith is traced in sand.

—WILLIAM E. AYTOUN, *LAYS OF THE SCOTTISH CAVALIERS* (1848)

And love beheld us from his secret stand,
    And mark'd his triumph, laughing, to behold me,
To see me trust a writing traced in sand,
    To see me credit what a woman told me.

—JORGE MONTEMÔR, *DIANA ENAMORADA* (ca. 1550)

■ *This insight, reasonably enough, has been incorporated into numerous legal codes.*

It was on account of her frivolity and because of the inconstancy of her sex and judgment that a woman was absolutely forbidden by the ancients to conduct a law-suit, to testify as a witness, or indeed to have anything to do with matters pertaining to the court.

—ROMAN LAW (A.D. 320)

In law . . . a hundred women are equal to only one witness.

—TALMUD, YEBAMOT 88B (ca. A.D. 300)

A child also cannot be made a witness in a court of law, nor a woman . . . nor a cheat. . . . These persons might give false evidence. A child would speak falsely from ignorance, a woman from want of veracity, an imposter from habitual depravity.

—NARADA, *THE SACRED LAWS* (HINDU SCRIPTURE, 4TH CENTURY A.D.)

■ *Not to be inflexible, our patriarchs did concede certain conditions under which a woman could bear witness.*

Every vow [by a woman], and every binding oath to affect the soul, her husband may establish it, or her husband may make it void.

—OLD TESTAMENT, NUMBERS 30:13 (ca. 500 B.C.)

We uphold the custom which, rectifying the errors of the law, denies women the right to give evidence. We hereby give this custom legal force and forbid women's evidence to be taken in matters concerned with contracts. But in purely feminine affairs, where men are not permitted to be present—I refer to childbirth and other things which only the female eye may see—women may testify.

—BYZANTINE LAW, BY EMPEROR LEO THE WISE, *NOVELS OF LEO* (ca. A.D. 900)

■ *As to the value men should place on counsel from women:*

Consult women, and do the opposite of what they advise.
—CALIPH OMAR I, SON-IN-LAW OF THE PROPHET MOHAMMAD (7TH CENTURY A.D.)

Husbands who consult their wives . . . are madmen if they think true prudence or good counsel lies within the female brain.
—LEON BATTISTA ALBERTI, ON *THE FAMILY* (15TH CENTURY)

Woman's counsel is fatal counsel.
—ENGLISH PROVERB (13TH CENTURY); ICELANDIC PROVERB

Nobody can influence me. Nobody at all. And a woman still less.
—REZA PAHLEVI, SHAH OF IRAN, INTERVIEW (1975)

For Women, with a mischief to their Kind,
Pervert, with bad Advice, our better Mind.
—JOHN DRYDEN, "THE COCK AND THE FOX" (1700)

Women are only children of a larger growth; they have an entertaining tattle, and sometimes wit, but for solid, reasoning good sense, I never in my life knew one that had it.
—LORD CHESTERFIELD, LETTER TO HIS SON (SEPTEMBER 5, 1748)

The generality of women appear to me as children whom I would rather give a sugar plum than my time.
—JOHN KEATS, LETTER TO GEORGE AND GEORGIANA KEATS (OCTOBER 21, 1818)

■ *In the end, women are weak because they are weak.*

Frailty, thy name is woman.
—HAMLET IN WILLIAM SHAKESPEARE, *HAMLET* (1601)

. . . She's but a woman,
As full of frailty as of faith, a poor slight woman,
And her best thoughts but weak fortifications.
—CHAMPERNEL IN BEAUMONT AND FLETCHER, *THE LITTLE FRENCH LAWYER* (1647)

As is the body, so is the soul of tender women frail.
—OVID, *HEROIDES* (ca. A.D. 10)

Nature has given horns to bulls, hoofs to horses, swiftness to hares, the power of swimming to fishes, of flying to birds, understanding to men. She had nothing left for women.
—ANACREON (ca. 500 B.C.)

Men have many faults, women only two:
Everything they say, and everything they do.
—ENGLISH PROVERB (17TH CENTURY)

■ *To sum up:*

You need only look at the way in which she is formed to see that woman is not meant to undergo great labor, whether of the mind or of the body. She pays the debt of life, not by what she does, but by what she suffers—by the pains of child-bearing and care for the child, and by submission to her husband, to whom she should be a patient and cheering companion. The keenest sorrows and joys are not for her, nor is she called upon to display a great deal of strength. The current of her life should be more gentle, peaceful and trivial than man's, without being essentially happier or unhappier.

Women are directly fitted for acting as the nurses and teachers of our early childhood, by the fact that they are themselves childish, frivo-

lous and shortsighted; in a word, they are big children all their life long
—a kind of intermediate stage between the child and the full-grown
male, who alone represents the *genus homo* in the strict sense of the
word. . . .

It is only the man whose intellect is clouded by his sexual impulses
that could give the name of *the fair sex* to that undersized, narrow-
shouldered, broad-hipped, and short-legged race; for the whole beauty
of the sex is bound up with this impulse. Instead of calling them beautiful, there would be more warrant for describing women as the
unesthetic sex. Neither for music, nor for poetry, nor for fine art,
have they really and truly any sense or susceptibility; it is a mere mockery if they make a pretense of it in order to assist their endeavor to
please. . . .

They form the *sexus sequior*—the second sex, inferior in every respect
to the first; their infirmities should be treated with consideration, but
to show them great reverence is extremely ridiculous, and lowers us in
their own eyes. . . .

That woman is by nature meant to obey may be seen by the fact that
every woman who is placed in the unnatural position of complete
independence, immediately attaches herself to some man by whom she
allows herself to be guided and ruled. It is because she needs a lord and
master. If she is young, it will be a lover; if she is old, a priest.

—ARTHUR SCHOPENHAUER, "ON WOMEN" (1851)

No mischief but a woman or a priest is at the bottom of it.

—LATIN PROVERB

And finally, woman! *One-half of mankind is weak,* chronically sick,
changeable, shifty—woman requires . . . a religion of the weak which
glorifies weakness, love and modesty as divine: or better still, she
makes the strong weak—she succeeds in overcoming the strong.

Woman has always conspired with decadent types—the priests, for instance—against the "mighty," against the "strong," against *men*. Women avail themselves of children for the cult of piety. . . .

—FRIEDRICH NIETZSCHE, *THE WILL TO POWER* (1888)

■ *We may sigh, along with the poet:*

O woman, you are not merely the handiwork of God, but also of men; these are ever endowing you with beauty from their own hearts. . . . You are one-half woman and one-half dream.

—RABINDRANATH TAGORE, *THE GARDENER* (ca. 1920)

■ *And yet, sadly enough:*

Women ever like to cover their foolishness with ingratitude.

—SPANISH PROVERB

■ *It seems, even after all this insight and analysis, that men remain confused:*

Such, Polly, are your sex—part truth, part fiction;
Some thought, much whim, and all a contradiction.

—RICHARD SAVAGE, "TO A YOUNG LADY" (1728)

And yet, believe me, good as well as ill.
Woman's at best a Contradiction still.
                    —ALEXANDER POPE, "OF THE CHARACTERS OF WOMEN" (1732–33)

■ *The great question remains:*

The great question that has never been answered and which I have not
yet been able to answer, despite my thirty years of research into the
feminine soul, is *What does a woman want?*
                    —SIGMUND FREUD, TO MARIE BONAPARTE (ca. 1935)

■ *Despite their apparent confusion, our patriarchs are ever ready to*
supply answers.

As much as women want to be good scientists and engineers, they
want, first and foremost, to be womanly companions of men and to
be mothers.
                    —DR. BRUNO BETTELHEIM, *WOMAN AND THE SCIENTIFIC PROFESSIONS* (1965)

The great ambition of women, believe me, is to inspire love.
                    —DOM PEDRE IN MOLIÈRE, *LE SICILIEN* (1667)

What all your sex desire is *Soveraignty*.
                    —JOHN DRYDEN, "THE WIFE OF BATH HER TALE" (1700)

In Men, we various Ruling Passions find;
In Women, two almost divide the kind;
Those, only fixed, they first or last obey,
The Love of Pleasure, and the Love of Sway.
                    —ALEXANDER POPE, "OF THE CHARACTERS OF WOMEN" (1732–33)

Woman is the same as horses: two wills act in opposition inside her. With one will, she wants to subject herself utterly. With the other, she wants to bolt, and pitch her rider to perdition.

—BIRKIN IN D. H. LAWRENCE, *WOMEN IN LOVE* (1920)

In truth, women of today, like the Valkyries of old, want anything but to win their fight for independence: the harder they fight, and the more bitchy they are, the more desperately they yearn for a man to be strong enough—for their man to be strong enough to limit them and to keep them from venting their destructiveness.

—WOLFGANG LEDERER, M.D., *THE FEAR OF WOMEN* (1968)

How did woman first become subject to man as she now is all over the world? By her nature, her sex, just as the negro is and always will be, to the end of time, inferior to the white race, and, therefore, doomed to subjection; but happier than she would be in any other condition, just because it is the law of her nature. The women themselves would not have this law reversed.

—EDITORIAL, *NEW YORK HERALD* (SEPTEMBER 12, 1852)

■ *After all:*

The generous sentiments of slaveholders are sufficient guarantee of the rights of woman, all the world over.

—GEORGE FITZHUGH, *SOCIOLOGY FOR THE SOUTH* (1854)

■ *But as in all matters dealing with women, a pessimist may well have the last word:*

I expect that woman will be the last thing civilized by man.

—GEORGE MEREDITH, *THE ORDEAL OF RICHARD FEVEREL* (1859)

Acknowledgments

Many individuals over the years have generously contributed the time, expertise, information, criticism, encouragement, and other intelligence that helped make this project become real. It would be impossible to thank them all, but special bouquets to: Lynn Chu, Laura Demanski, Michael Hart, Glen Hartley, Robert Herrmann, Marcia Kurop, Martha Lambert, Alexandra Mullen, Ann Patty, Elaine Pfefferblit (my editor at Poseidon Press), Charles Portney, Jennifer Tolbert Roberts, Roberta Rosenthal (who found the witty and wonderful illustrations), staff of the Hawaii State Library System, staff of the San Francisco Public Library, Jean Starr, Jonathan Starr, Dhyana Sylvian, Tina Christenfeld Weiner, and the anonymous team of geniuses in Orem, Utah, who invented WordPerfect 5.1.

Grateful acknowledgment is made to the following for permission to reprint illustrations:

Chapter 2, page 41: The Bettmann Archive.

Chapter 3, page 51: Reprinted by permission from *Period*. Copyright © 1979, 1981, 1991 by JoAnn Gardner-Loulan, Bonnie Lopez, and Marcia Quackenbush. Illustrations copyright © 1979 by Marcia Quackenbush. Volcano Press, Inc., P.O. Box 271, Volcano, CA 95689. (209) 296-3445.

Chapter 3, page 55: by Tama Starr.

Chapter 4, page 62: by Thomas Petts. Reprinted from *Against Women: A Satire* by permission of Associated University Presses.

Chapter 4, page 65: by Jill Schwarz. Reprinted by permission of the artist.

Chapter 6, page 107: by Tama Starr.

Chapter 9, page 143: by Sona Gumusyan. Reprinted by permission of the artist.

Chapter 9, pages 146–47: The Bettmann Archive.

Chapter 9, page 149: by Thomas Petts. Reprinted from *Against Women: A Satire* by permission of Associated University Presses.

Chapter 10, page 162: The Bettmann Archive.

Index

About the Author

Tama Starr is President of the Artkraft Strauss Sign Corporation, which lights up Broadway, New York City's "Great White Way." This is her first book.